The Shawlies: Cork's women street traders and the 'merchant city', 1901–50

Maynooth Studies in Local History

SERIES EDITOR Raymond Gillespie

This volume is one of six short books published in the Maynooth Studies in Local History series in 2017. Like their predecessors they range widely, both chronologically and geographically, over the local experience in the Irish past. Chronologically they span the worlds of early modern Kerry, 18th-century Stradbally, in Laois, and those of Dublin and Cork in the early 20th century. Geographically they range across the length of the country from Dublin to Cork and westwards to the Atlantic world of Kerry. Socially they move from the landed and elite society of Castle Hyde and Stradbally Hall to the social position of the 20th-century Cork women street traders and Dublin tenement dwellers and examining the experience of the rising middle class in Fingal. In doing so they reveal diverse and complicated societies that created the local past and present the range of possibilities open to anyone interested in studying that past. Those possibilities involve the dissection of the local experience in the complex and contested social worlds of which it is part as people strove to preserve and enhance their positions within their local societies. Such studies of local worlds over such long periods are vital for the future since they not only stretch the historical imagination but provide a longer perspective on the evolution of society in Ireland and help us to understand more fully the complex evolution of the Irish experience. These works do not simply chronicle events relating to an area within administrative or geographically determined boundaries, but open the possibility of understanding how and why particular regions had their own personality in the past. Such an exercise is clearly one of the most exciting challenges for the future and demonstrates the vitality of the study of local history in Ireland.

Like their predecessors, these six short books are reconstructions of the socially diverse worlds of the poor as well as the rich, women as well as men, the geographical marginal as well as those located near the centre of power. They examine the way in which those who inhabited those worlds lived their daily lives, often little affected by the large themes that dominate the writing of national history. In addressing these issues, studies such as those presented in these short books, together with their predecessors, are at the forefront of Irish historical research and represent some of the most innovative and exciting work being undertaken in Irish history today. They also provide models which others can follow up and adapt in their own studies of the Irish past. In such ways will we understand better the regional diversity of Ireland and the social and cultural basis for that diversity. These books, with their predecessors, convey the vibrancy and excitement of the world of Irish local history today.

Maynooth Studies in Local History: Number 131

The Shawlies: Cork's women street traders and the 'merchant city', 1901–50

Susan Marie Martin

FOUR COURTS PRESS

Set in 10pt on 12pt Bembo by
Carrigboy Typesetting Services for
FOUR COURTS PRESS LTD
7 Malpas Street, Dublin 8, Ireland
www.fourcourtspress.ie
and in North America for
FOUR COURTS PRESS
c/o ISBS, 920 N.E. 58th Avenue, Suite 300, Portland, OR 97213

ISBN 978–1–84682–644–3

Printed in Ireland
by SprintPrint, Dublin.

Contents

Acknowledgments

I am most grateful to Dr Jacqui O'Riordan and Dr Máire Leane for their ongoing creative support; I am not certain that this project would have emerged as it did without their help. I am also grateful to Professor Maria Luddy and Professor Linda Connolly for suggestions and encouragement. Thanks are due to Brian McGee and the staff of the Cork City and County Archives for their support, encouragement, and for going above and beyond to locate materials from disparate corners of the collection that pieced together this story. As ever, I thank Fergus for his patience and for making life that much better. Eternal thanks are due to my Nana, Eileen Mary Mulholland, for passing on a love of Cork's stories and its streets, a love of reading, and a desire to right social wrongs.

Introduction

On the eve of Ireland's 1901 census, Corkonian Mary Carlton, aged 18 years, was rearing and supporting herself, her 16-year-old sister and her 12-year-old brother. She had taken in a lodger, aged 17 years, presumably to help pay the rent on the two rooms they were living in – housing considered unfit for human habitation. Both Mary and her sister Eliza were selling onions on the streets of Cork, her brother John sold newspapers, and their lodger, Mary Donoghue, worked as a domestic. Employment on the margins of the economy, as well as the extra-familial living arrangement, would, possibly, help to keep them all out of the poor house. Such employment was frequently termed 'an honest living' because the alternative for women and girls for whom the basics of daily survival were so precarious was prostitution. Mary and Eliza counted among the 23 women who listed their occupation in Ireland's 1901 census as 'onion seller'. There were no onion sellers listed in another city or town in Ireland. They, like so many women, had dominated street trade in Ireland for centuries. However, it was typically shopkeepers or 'bricks and mortar' traders with assets and property holdings that had social and political power, and it is those traders who left some tangible historical traces.

Those who left pronounced traces on Cork's cityscape from the 18th century onwards would later become known collectively as the 'merchant princes'. Having made their fortunes in the provisions trade, they dominated the city's political, social and cultural life. At the opening of the 20th century, power was, however, shifting to firm-based commercial interests and away from the provisions trade. In 1901, as Mary Carlton was selling onions on the streets, Cork's lord mayor, Edward Fitzgerald, announced that the city would host an international industrial exhibition. It opened in May 1902 to such success it was re-staged in 1903. It attracted exhibitors and visitors from around the world, including royalty. King Edward VII and Queen Alexandra attended, and later honoured Fitzgerald with a baronetcy. The century may have opened with the promise of 'progress', but a significant portion of the city's population was, like Mary Carlton, struggling. In the 1911 census, no one reported their profession as 'onion seller'; however, hundreds of women continued to survive by selling fruit, vegetables, meat, fish, second-hand clothing, small wares, and sources of fuel on the streets of Cork, most of them crowded into the neglected medieval city centre where they also lived. Five years on, in 1916, the Report of the Medical Superintendent Officer of Health announced that approximately one-ninth of Cork's population, 8,675 persons, were living in 719 tenements, including 2,928 families. According to the report, many housing spaces that were originally designed for a single family were housing several.[1]

A great concentration of tenements was found in the medieval city centre surrounding Corn Market Street and North Main Street. The ubiquity of poor and working-class women, known locally as 'the Shawlies', who dominated trading in the open market place of Cork's Corn Market Street emerges from photographs taken in the opening decades of the 20th century. Corn Market Street, known locally as 'the Coal Quay', stands in local memory as a place belonging to them, although there were eras when they traded at other locations. However, they were not always welcome elsewhere and were, as early as the 18th century, presented as deviant and hazards on the thoroughfares. In 1786, when Cork's local authority created a Market Jury, later the Tolls and Markets Committee (TMC), one of the stated goals was to deal with substandard hygiene in the city's regulated open markets, but they also set out to regulate the 'Fruit Women' and 'Green Women' who sold in the meat market and on bridges. They were said to be 'very great Nuisances and Obstructions'.[2] They toiled in the periphery of the retail economy and, through such characterizations, were pushed even further into the social margins. Despite this, Cork's poor and working-class women continued to dominate street sales at stalls and as itinerant traders into the 19th and 20th centuries.

To understand why these women entered work in the margins of Cork's retail economy, and sought out work often characterized by those in power as socially deviant, one must look through both historical and contemporary studies of women street traders, and studies of the historical limits that hampered an Irish woman's chances in the mainstream economy. The number of women employed in 'white collar' professions such as teaching, nursing or administrative positions may have increased significantly after 1850, but they remained a minority at only 5 per cent of Ireland's female population in 1911.[3] From 1880 through 1918, women's work was concentrated in agriculture, domestic service and work in textiles,[4] three sectors vulnerable to changes in the larger economy, and technological changes across time. The advent of creameries, for example, significantly reduced a traditional source of earnings for women on large dairy farms.[5] In the textile industry, the number of women who were employed as 'spinners' and 'weavers' across Ireland was reduced by 79 per cent between 1851 and 1911.[6] The census records compiled in Ireland between 1881 and 1911 reveal that the number employed in the traditional area of domestic service declined by approximately 13 per cent.[7] More generally, girls and women who were listed as 'gainfully' employed on the census taken in 1911 dropped to 19.5 per cent from 28 per cent in 1851.[8] Those classified as negligibly employed or unemployed increased on every census between 1881 and 1911, with a net increase of approximately 17 per cent.[9] By 1926, when the Street Trading Act was brought into law, 60 per cent of working Irish women were employed in the traditionally female friendly sectors of agriculture or domestic service[10] – however, the unemployment rate in those two sectors was by then 17 per cent.[11]

These figures demonstrate that economic vulnerability and finding a way to survive in the Irish economy was a pressing concern for women into the opening decades of the 20th century. In Cork a gender line had, historically, existed among the economically vulnerable. In 1846, women made up 74 per cent of the Cork union workhouse population and remained in the majority as the percentages of able-bodied women who sought refuge remained consistent with that recorded during the Famine.[12] Data on employment, unemployment and poverty, as well as a closer look at domestic and agricultural work, are critical to a study of women street traders in order to determine why they were compelled to earn in the streets. Historically and globally, women who have been made vulnerable by the lack of opportunities for women, or those too old or frail to handle the demands of domestic labour, often turn to street trading – despite its precarious earnings – as their only means for survival.[13] Contemporary studies have found that in an economy where a significant number of women are employed as domestics and competition is fierce, their chances of finding work are reduced, and are further amplified when the agricultural sector is in decline, forcing more women to move to cities in search of work as domestics.[14]

For a woman who turned to Cork's streets to trade, or entered a custom maintained by her mother and grandmother, the work may have been marginal, but it was legal. The term 'street trader' came into existence as an official descriptor in the 1920s. Prior to that they were 'pedlars', and the legislation that governed their trade until 1926 was the Pedlars' Act, 1871. A pedlar required a licence and traded on foot, selling goods or providing services such as sewing and mending. Those who sold food such as vegetables, fish, fruit or victuals, however, did not require a licence. An additional exemption was also granted to those who sold goods of any kind in a public market place or a fair that was legally established. This was, in short, an individual's 'market right'. Cork had, historically, designated areas where small traders such as the Shawlies could freely sell goods. Corn Market Street, from the early years of the 20th century, had an exemption to laws on obstruction, a sanction of sorts for street sales provided by the local authority.[15] The changes in the social and political order that followed Irish independence in 1922 would, however, change the trading lives of the Shawlies, and the public marketplace. The democratic agency of these women was, essentially, negated by both the local authority and the Irish Free State government: regulation of their work, under the Street Trading Act, 1926, facilitated the power of private interests to dictate the uses of public space at the expense of the city's neediest citizens.

My study of both the Shawlies and the design and implementation of this legislation reveals that social inequality, including gendered poverty, was perpetuated by men in power who simply reconstructed the 'truth' of what constituted social ills in public spaces. These ills were now identified as blocked footpaths, slow flows of vehicular traffic and litter. Failing to create opportunities for women to earn in the mainstream economy was not perceived as a shortcoming of those who governed; however, failing to respond to the demands of shopkeepers and larger firms, or to follow the dictates of patriarchal town planners was construed as a failure of governance. In the official discourse at municipal and state levels, men holding political power had, seemingly, a moral obligation to serve the merchant class and those lobbying for an economy that favoured the larger business interests in the new Irish state. In the midst of this discourse, women street traders were rendered deviant socially, morally and, later, criminally. Mary Carlton would no longer be a young, destitute guardian. Instead, she and the other Shawlies would be conceptualized as active, willing sources of dirt and disorder in Cork's modern city centre, and sources of contagion and fraud unwilling to 'play fair' with ratepayers. In a newly independent Ireland, the solution deemed 'sensible' and 'fair' was regulation that spelled their removal from the public space. The government professed to lend legitimacy to their work, but instead allowed for women street traders to be pushed further into the margins of Irish society and the economy.

This piece of local history began as a doctoral study that was interdisciplinary in nature, crossing the academic 'boundaries' of sociology, social policy, and governance. An interdisciplinary approach was vital to understanding the workings of the Street Trading Act, 1926. It is my intention in this study to demonstrate what I learned early on: namely, how the power of a seemingly innocuous piece of legislation was galvanized through a re-articulation of trading activity by vested interests, both male and middle class. This type of power does not have an apex but moves through social interactions and positions individuals in society. This work is an interrogation of mundane regulations, and their connection to the 'visionary' elements at work in the new Irish state and the city of Cork in the years following Irish independence. It documents a portion of Cork's social history, and how strategies of governance, including regulation, policy and urban planning, deepened the marginalization of women who were already socially and economically marginalized. This provides a new lens through which to view what happens when pre-existing social conditions in Cork meet historical events that, on the surface, appear far removed; these include the push by amalgamated business interests for a modern town plan that privileged industry and commercial interests, the dissolution of the Cork Corporation, the reformation of local authorities across Ireland, and the struggle by various business interests to control the agenda of the Irish Free State government.

Although it is important that these questions about power, privilege and the foundation of the state be addressed, this is not the only intention behind this study. Indeed, the 'meta intention' is to emancipate, as much as possible, the lives and the work of the Shawlies. Michel Foucault contended that it is through creating a genealogy that the researcher gives life to subjugated narratives, voices and knowledge – by reactivating the voices of those opposed to this coercion by the privileged and powerful.[16] This book, then, is a contribution to the growing body of work that documents Irish social history, Irish women's history and, more importantly, the history of poor Irish women who have remained largely invisible. Their adaptation to, and exploitation of, their situations make them women who are conceptualized as 'active agents in the historical process'.[17] That said, their place in recorded history has remained, to this point, a blank despite their ubiquity in photographs and local histories documenting life in Cork.

Thus, establishing a genealogy of processes, institutions and legislation through disparate sources was critical to the creation of this very local history. Statistics do not establish the context in which numbers are produced: demographic variables collected in a census simply make a population known to its government as numbers and subjects to be governed. For this reason, early 20th-century sociological studies in Britain provided more direction for research when used in conjunction with interviews to supplement the numbers.[18] Thus, I have employed qualitative research methods, drawing on discourses available in documentary sources, and quantitative research methods to compile demographical profiles of the Shawlies using information gathered from the 1901 and 1911 census forms, and a registry of street traders that was compiled by Gardaí in 1928. The discourses available included government sources at the national level: relevant legislation, both pre- and post-independence, and the debates database of the Oireachtas. Locally, the minutes of the committees and the council of Cork Corporation from 1900 through to 1946 were used. A business plan for the city, published in 1918, along with the planning documents of 1926 and 1941, helped develop this genealogy and establish the larger social context surrounding the push to regulate street trading. While this work did produce a significant amount of data, there were some gaps in the public debates. This led me to search for newspaper accounts to determine how the Act was perceived, and how street trading was regarded publicly. The digitized *Irish Times*, Ireland's newspaper of public record, was used to search for articles about the Act's design and implementation both in Dublin and in Cork. This helped to reconstruct the public narrative that construed street trading as deviant.

The situation in Cork was not detailed in the debates at the national level. The absence of this information made it difficult to determine why legislation that was intended to address what was characterized nationally as a problem in Dublin became a problem in Cork. For this reason, documents publicly available at the Cork City and County Archives were consulted. A file of correspondence and memoranda pertaining to street trading and the implementation of the Act in Cork became the central documentary source of information for this study. This file also contains the original registry compiled by Gardaí. At places where there appeared to be gaps in the meta-narrative generated by the council and committee minutes, the *Cork Examiner*, Cork's newspaper of public record in that era, was consulted. Issues of the newspaper immediately preceding and following all the council and committee meetings where street trading was on the agenda were consulted to fill in any blanks. According to one researcher, it is dangerous to assume that the most important data is the available data, without considering how it was collected, and the social context in which that data was produced.[19] This proviso proved invaluable throughout the initial study, and on subsequent visits to the Cork City and County Archives. Accepting only the data that was readily available as the most important would not allow for an honest telling of this story. Thus, by constantly questioning the context in which that data was produced, I believe that I have overcome the core limitations of documentary research that could leave many voices silent.

Many stereotypes of street traders exist that have become 'truth' as they have been recounted across time and space. One that persists in Cork and globally is that some street traders become wealthy through the low overheads that such trading generates, as well as by avoiding taxes. This is not the reality of the women whose lives are documented here, nor is it the reality for their sisters globally. In his autobiography *It's a long way from penny apples*, Irish businessman Bill Cullen credits his time as a youngster helping his mother and maternal grandmother, both Dublin street traders, with honing the business acumen that would allow him to find macroeconomic wealth in the late 20th century. Indeed, Cullen foregrounds the economic and social challenges that motivated women like his mother and grandmother, whether widowed or married, to trade and provide vital flows of cash for the family's survival. That there are so many photographs of a teeming Corn Market Street, and of women selling elsewhere in Cork, is telling; these photographs are a testament to the existence of these street traders, and are visual representations of the very public failure of the social and political powers to create survival alternatives for women who lived and toiled in the social, economic and political margins.

In September 1924, when moves to ban street trading in Cork were heightened, a solicitor said to be representing approximately 500 traders, told the Hackney Carriages Committee (HCC) that a ban would inflict a tremendous hardship on those with no choice but to trade in the street, as they had for decades, and would further impoverish the traders and their families.[20] Speaking before the same committee, the solicitor representing Musgrave Brothers Ltd, a wholesale grocer seeking to have street trading banned, labelled women street traders, including 'onion sellers', as obstructions to business interests he characterized as 'normal' and 'valid'.[21] Nearly a century later, in a note of historical irony, a memorial of sorts to the Shawlies was placed on the west side of Corn Market Street by the local authority in June 2012; it stands facing the refurbished facade of the Musgrave Buildings. This bronze statue, sculpted by Seamus Murphy, immortalizes an aged, tired-looking woman, head covered and body wrapped in her shawl. Her name was Mary Anne.[22] The plaque on the base identifies her as 'the onion seller'.

1. 'A chaos of sittings, standings, and stalls': the Shawlies in Cork's retail core and periphery

To understand the challenges confronting the Shawlies, it is important to tell the tale of two neighbourhoods – St Patrick's Street and North Main Street – and how political and social power shaped those two 'worlds'. The significance of the two locations is demonstrated by the public funds devoted to gentrification efforts in the city centre across more than 200 years, as well as the image of each neighbourhood in relation to the common perception of what constitutes a modern city – order, efficiency and the 'new'.[1] This modernist 'ideal' was embraced locally by both the political and business elites from the 18th through to the 20th century. In current economic terms, St Patrick's Street came to form the retail 'core', while North Main Street stood on the 'periphery' of wealth and power. A closer look at both neighbourhoods and the trade carried on in them reveals that each also had its own margin or periphery, with the 'bricks and mortar' traders representing the core, and the streets and footpaths serving as the periphery.

THE MERCHANT CITY

An old, established urban centre with waterways and a port, surrounded by rich farmlands, Cork city was, by the 18th century, dotted with a large number of small, open-air markets for the sale and purchase of food, all regulated by the Corporation. Many were located in the laneways running off from North Main Street, the city centre since medieval times. Spaces were rented to vendors by the Corporation, and activity was regulated through inspections that included the calibration of scales and hygiene. In addition to the open markets, the Corporation permitted street trading by independent, mobile traders or pedlars. The Corporation minutes of 16 November 1756 record that a trader could pitch a stall and sell from that place for 30 minutes without having to pay a fee to the Corporation. The items that could be sold represents the staples of daily life: fuel, fowl, straw, wool, brooms, oysters and oats.[2]

Cork's macro-economy was based on the trade generated by the city's location on the trans-Atlantic trade routes, and the bountiful agricultural economy that surrounded it. Cork was the world's largest exporter of butter, enjoyed across the British Empire. Cork was also a key supplier of pork and beef to the British Navy. It is not surprising, then, that the city was dominated, socially and politically, by its wealthy merchant class, known later as the 'merchant princes'. Cork itself would later adopt the moniker 'the Merchant City'.[3] In this period, these men amalgamated to create a Committee of Merchants that influenced political decisions.[4] Such was their power that public funds were earmarked by the local authority to reconfigure the social and economic landscape of the city. As a result, St Patrick's Street, anchoring the current city centre, was created in the years approaching the 19th century. After its establishment, many middle-class merchants relocated their businesses there, moving from the medieval city centre. This movement, and the building of high-status residences nearby, made the new city centre the residence, workplace and retail locale of choice for the professional and merchant classes. Its popularity and growth raised the call for a food market in the area to serve the gentry.[5] The Corporation responded, again with public funds, and constructed a covered food market located off St Patrick's Street and the Grand Parade, now the south end of the internationally recognized English Market.

Just as the wealthy retail core was, evidently, reserved for the upper classes, it was also a gendered location that favoured the men who owned and operated its retail establishments. Middle and upper class women were evident as customers, but the census returns detailing ownership of retail premises and residences on St Patrick's Street reveal that working women were, typically, domestic servants or, in trade terms, 'drapers' assistants' rather than 'drapers'.[6] Within the Grand Parade Market, the power of the collective voice of the male-dominated butchers' trade union dictated much of the market's life through to the mid-20th century, and the women who did trade there as butchers were typically widows assuming the business after the death of a spouse, or women with a family connection to a man who had held the butcher's stall.[7] The Shawlies who did trade in that core traded in what was then the open-air Princes Street Market at the north end of the Grand Parade Market. While its location may have been 'high-end', conditions put it a world away from the genteel covered market.

Created in the early 1790s by the Corporation for the sale of poultry and vegetables, the Princes Street Market was described as a 'chaos of standings, sittings and stalls', on a mud floor, in contrast to the covered market where rents were much higher.[8] Women also dominated trade on Princes Street at the entrance to the market. They were labelled a nuisance, a hazard, and even criminal: an article in the *Cork Constitution* in 1858 accused women traders of making the thoroughfare impassable and suggested that the women aided pickpockets.[9] The Princes Street Market remained open to the elements until the 1860s. Pressure for improvements began late in 1861, but nothing materialized. A letter of complaint published in the *Cork Examiner* prompted a visit by the lord mayor. The letter described a setting without gaslight, one where business could not be conducted at night when the main Grand Parade Market remained open and lit. This fact presented circumstances the correspondent called unjust, acknowledging the contribution of these women 'to the public revenues of

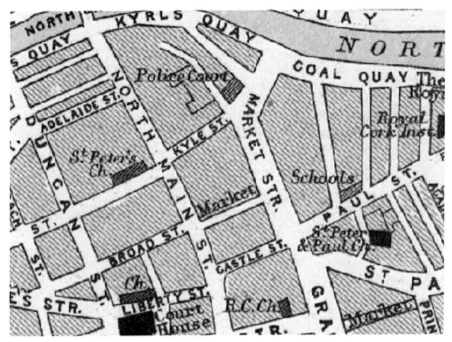

1. Map of market area, Cork, 1903

the city'.[10] The refurbished, covered market was opened in December 1862, and the official ceremony to open it was recorded in the *Cork Examiner*. The correspondent described the women traders sympathetically as the 'legitimate lords of the soil', those with the most to gain by an improved market.[11]

THE SHAWLIES AND THE MEDIEVAL CITY CENTRE

On the cusp of the 20th century, street trading remained a significant occupation for women and girls. By 1891, 14.1 per cent of women in Cork were dealing, and in the census of 1901 the percentage of women dealing reached its highest proportion of occupations recorded on all census returns from 1841: 19 per cent of the city's female population were now identified as dealers.[12] However, it is likely that the majority were trading in the medieval city centre, where North Main Street now anchored what had become, largely, a neighbourhood for the impoverished and the working classes. The creation and gentrification of St Patrick's Street had sparked, in turn, the degeneration of the medieval city and the 'Coal Quay', and it is there that the Shawlies were largely contained, away from the privileged retail core.

In 1842, attempts were made by the local authority to improve the lot of those who lived and traded on the Coal Quay; funds were designated to build the covered markets of St Peter's and the Bazaar on North Main Street, backing on to Corn Market Street. Locally, a notable affection for the neighbourhood has remained, despite the rowdy reputation it had had since the early 19th century. This was largely because it was home to many unlicensed pubs.[13] In 1907, the journalist William Bulfin visited Corn Market Street during a tour of Ireland, and his account confirms local affection for the marketplace. He recounted how he had first learned of it from a Cork man during a conversation held over coffee in a city far away – presumably in Argentina, Bulfin's country of residence. His companion described the Coal Quay as commercially important, but the only marketplace he knew of where one's handkerchief could be stolen upon entry, and sold back to its owner at the exit. When Bulfin admonished his companion for this negative depiction, he was told that a native was permitted to joke thus, but those from outside Cork were not; thus, the Corkman cautioned, if Bulfin wrote about 'Paddy's Market', he should 'bear my words in mind'.[14] Interestingly, Bulfin characterized the Coal Quay as an 'open-air institution', a testament to the life and scale of this marketplace: it was then home to jobbers, small shops, 'eating-house proprietors',[15] and approximately 11 public houses and nine refreshment rooms.[16]

Street trading may have been tolerated here because it was contained within the neighbourhood: complaints about street traders in the public record were sporadic and did not receive a lot of attention from the local authority. The HCC employed street inspectors to investigate obstructions, and the committee's minutes, from the early 20th century through to 1929 when it was dissolved, reveal that cases of obstruction were, typically, complaints involving large-scale obstructions caused by businesses referred to consistently as 'firms', rather than obstructions by the Shawlies. Likewise, the TMC minutes from the early 20th century until it was dissolved in 1929 reveal few complaints. As noted in the introduction, the HCC did grant an exemption in 1902 regarding street obstructions on Corn Market Street, from an order of the Constabulary; however, North Main Street, a major retail thoroughfare for 'bricks and mortar' traders, was not given this exemption, and it would remain a focus for complaints from merchants across the coming decades.

After a complaint against the sale of used clothing on North Main Street was made to the HCC by the stallholders in the Bazaar Market in June 1904, on 8 August a letter from a solicitor representing women described as 'poor' and selling goods on North Main Street was read at the HCC. He reported that his clients were forced on to the street when their goods were not selling in the Bazaar Market. He asked that they be allowed to trade on North Main Street in the vicinity of the markets, but the HCC decided that the Corporation could not sanction trading in the open on North Main Street. On 26 September 1904, a recommendation that originated at council was read at the HCC requesting that all complaints of obstruction in North Main Street be reviewed, and to prosecute accordingly. The HCC decided to prosecute all who caused an obstruction, excepting apple vendors. A similar sympathy for women trading in the open was demonstrated in May 1905 when a solicitor appeared before the HCC on behalf of women who had been charged with obstruction on Corn Market Street for selling fish, fruit and vegetables. The exemption that had been granted in 1902 was not mentioned. That said, the HCC seemed sympathetic to the women – it deferred consideration for three months with a view to finding alternate arrangements for them.[17]

However, in October 1905, a councillor resurrected the complaint on behalf of shopkeepers in North Main Street against those selling milk, butter and eggs from carts, alleging interference with their trade. It was noted that the Constabulary had been ordered to prevent street trading, but had not been successful. The Street Inspector was ordered to end it. The issue remained muted for another two years. On 27 February 1907, a solicitor representing residents and shopkeepers in North Main Street complained to the HCC of obstructions by women street traders who were selling second-hand clothing and bedding. This complaint is significant for its negative construction of the women. It alleged that they deterred customers from coming to North Main Street because they shook their old goods and scattered dust that was 'offensive' and 'possibly infectious'. It was revisited in the following April; however, further action was deferred. If the local authority did not appear keen to take action in this matter, the shopkeepers in North Main Street were concerned, according to a story in the *Irish Times* on 26 July 1909. At the time, they were reported to have attended the courts and requested a restraining order against the women, alleging they were a 'public nuisance'. The shopkeepers alleged their trade had been damaged because old bedding, clothes, and 'rubbishy articles' were placed for sale on the thoroughfare, producing 'insanitary odours' to the 'prejudice' of both the public and the shopkeepers. The women did not appear, and an injunction was granted.

WHO WERE THE SHAWLIES?

Not unlike the women selling used items in North Main Street at the turn of the century, girls and women designated as 'onion sellers' were also described as delinquent nuisances when they sold in and around the English Market,[18] and later in the 1920s when they sold in the vicinity of Corn Market Street. Who were these girls and women who sold onions and used clothing on the streets of Cork? Why did they present threats to larger traders and the firm-based economy? It is these groups of women street traders who reveal the economic vulnerability of poor and working-class women.

A search of the census returns for 1901 was made with only the term 'onion' in the occupation field; the gender and county fields were left blank.

The results from the 1901 census reveal that the 'onion seller' was, potentially, a phenomenon unique to Cork: only 23 citizens declared their occupation to be 'onion vendor', all were women and all lived in Cork city. They all lived in four lanes running off Corn Market Street: Curtis Lane, Albert Row, Fitzgerald's Alley and Harpur's Lane. In some homes, more than one woman was an onion seller. The eldest was 70 years of age, and the youngest was aged 13 years. The demographics culled from the census for this group of women indicate a desperate need to earn: of that number, 16 were unmarried, four were widowed, and the remaining three were married but not living with a spouse. Five were head of a household with dependents, and 20 were contributing to the family economy, 11 were part of a family with a female head of household. It is evident from these numbers that a significant number of women were supporting themselves and others simply by selling onions to passers-by.

Other personal particulars point to their economic vulnerability. Of the 23, 13 were aged less than 20 years, and two were aged 60–70 years. Only seven had such basic literacy skills as would typically increase one's chances of finding gainful employment; 70 per cent could not read or write. The earnings were particularly significant to young women: approximately 83 per cent were under the age of 25. The scattering of the remaining four women across age groups, and the gaps in age after 25 years suggest that onion selling was a tenuous form of street trading, particularly when considered alongside the information on marital status and the number of onion sellers who were the head of their household. This may have been work that was taken on when women could not access more stable forms of street trading. The figures on housing status indicate conclusively that onion selling was a means of survival for the economically marginalized: all resided in tenements, and a significant number, 74 per cent, resided in tenements considered unfit for human habitation. Approximately 13 per cent were lodgers.

The numbers above demonstrate the necessity of allowing these women to trade on the streets in order to house themselves and their families, and illustrate the dependence of poor families upon street trading at a very basic level, even when a male earner was the head of household. It is clear, too, that onion selling was a profession shaped by both class and gender. The following narrative, culled from the 1901 census data, provides a closer look at the home lives of the twenty-three onion sellers, and gives life to the women who comprised these figures.

For widows, with or without dependents, onion selling was a vital source of income. Julia Barry, 60, was a widow living with her three adult children. She and her son, 19, a labourer, were literate. However, her 15-year-old daughter, a scholar, could not read, nor could her 22-year-old daughter, a domestic servant. They lived in two rooms. Annie Eyers, 40, was also a widow. Her daughter Margaret, 16, was also an onion seller. They resided with Annie's other daughter, 13 years of age and attending school, and a female lodger, 18, who was a domestic servant. Both Annie and the lodger were illiterate, but Margaret and her sister were literate. They lived in two rooms. Ellen Spillane, 30, was also widowed. Both she and her daughter Ellen, 15, were onion sellers, and both were illiterate. They lived in one room. Mary Barry, 70, was a widow who lived alone. She was illiterate.

Onion sellers also supported their widowed mothers. Mary Ellen Murray, 17, and her half-sister, Maggie Barry, 13, were both onion sellers. Both were illiterate. Their mother, 43, was also illiterate and worked as a rag picker. She also had a 5-year-old son. They lived in two rooms. Mary Costello, 18, was the sole earner in a family of seven. Her mother, aged 42 years and widowed, was raising Mary and her five siblings, aged 14 down to 3 years of age; Mary's siblings were in school. Mary's mother was illiterate, while Mary and all but her two youngest siblings could read only. They lived in one room. Julia Cotter, 15, was literate; she resided with her mother, 46 and widowed, an older sister, and a female lodger. Her mother did not work outside the home; her sister was employed as a tobacco spinner. The lodger was a rag picker. Julia and her sister were literate; her mother and the lodger were not. They lived in one room. Mary O'Brien, 23, and Catherine O'Brien, 19, were supporting themselves and their widowed mother, 48, who did not work outside the home. All were illiterate. They lived in two rooms.

In one case, two onion sellers played a vital role in a family economy where a married woman was the head of a household, but her spouse was not in the home. Margaret Walsh, 23, and her sister Hannah Cleary lived with their 46-year-old mother who did not work outside the home. Like her mother, Margaret was married, but was not residing with her spouse. Margaret and Hannah also helped support three younger siblings. Their two brothers, 12 and 10, were employed as newsvendors. They also had an 8-year-old sister who was in school. All were illiterate. These six people lived in two rooms.

Onion sellers played an important role in the family economy even when a male was the head of household. Kathleen Sweeney, 20, was married but lived with her parents and siblings. Her father, a foreman, and her mother, who did not work outside the home, were both illiterate. Kathleen's brothers, 14 and 10, were newsvendors. Her youngest brother, aged 8, was not in school and was illiterate. Kathleen and her two working brothers were literate. They lived in three rooms. Margaret O'Brien, 18, lived with her father, a labourer, her mother, and six siblings. Her mother did not work outside the home; her older brother was a labourer. Only Margaret and three of her siblings were literate. This family of nine lived in two rooms. Margaret Daly, 19, was literate. She lived with her mother and father; he was employed but his occupation is illegible. Margaret's younger sister, 11, was in school. Mary O'Neill, 18, lodged with the family. She, too, was an onion seller. All were literate. They lived in two rooms.

For single women like Mary O'Neill, or married women not living with their spouses, onion selling was their sole means of support. Like Mary, Margaret Barry, 19, was a lodger residing with a fisherman and his wife. Unlike

Mary, she was illiterate. These three adults lived in one room. Julia Field, 22, was married but lived alone in two rooms. She could not read. Ellen Broaderick, 20, was married but lived alone. She was illiterate. Ellen Crowley, 21, and her sister, Kate Crowley, 18, were both illiterate. They lived alone in three rooms. The story of Mary Carlton was told in the introduction.

The following sample of women traders was selected from those who named their occupation as a dealer in 'clothes', 'old clothes' or 'second-hand clothes'. Accused by shopkeepers of cutting into profits because customers were turned off by the offensive odours and the potential spread of infectious diseases from their goods, who were these women who allegedly threatened business and public health? A search of the census returns for 1901 and 1911 was made with the search terms 'clothes' in the occupation field and Cork in the county field; the gender was left at 'both'. In the 1901 census, 75 names were returned for Cork, but four persons were eliminated because they were involved in the commercial sale of clothing. In the 1911 census, 42 names were returned for Cork city. Like onion selling, this too was a profession shaped by class and gender across both censuses. Of the 71 clothes dealers recorded in 1901, only nine were men, and only one of them lived in the DED of the medieval city centre selected for this study's random sample. This meant that 45 women, or 63 per cent of the total number of clothes dealers, lived in the medieval city centre. Of the 42 clothes dealers recorded in 1911, all were women, suggesting that 'clothes dealer' may have become even more gendered across the decade. Of the 42 women recorded in 1911, 33 or 79 per cent resided in those same DEDs suggesting, once again, that this profession was shaped by social class.

Across both samples, it is difficult to determine if these women worked in the Bazaar Market or on the street, because where they sold was rarely recorded. However, regardless of status, commonalities among the women named do emerge, including some commonalities with the onion sellers. In 1901, a significant number of these women, 42 per cent, were widowed; that number, although still significant, was reduced to 21 per cent in the 1911 sample. The number of unmarried women in the profession was fairly consistent, 36 per cent and 43 per cent in 1901 and 1911 respectively. A woman clothes dealer, it would appear, stood to have more domestic stability than an onion seller. Like the onion sellers, a significant number of clothes dealers in both 1901 and 1911 were contributing to a family economy: 62 per cent of the clothes dealers in the 1901 sample, a number that rose to 88 per cent in the 1911 sample. Unlike the onion sellers, though, a clothes dealer was more likely to be residing in a family with a male head of household; among those who were married, a clothes dealer was also more likely to be residing with her spouse. The number of women who were married but not living with the spouse was only 4 per cent and 9 per cent among the clothes dealers in 1901 and 1911 respectively. While 31 per cent were head of household with dependents in 1901, and 24 per cent were head of household with dependents in 1911, 36 per cent resided in a home with a male head of household in 1901. This number rose considerably to 58 per cent of the clothes dealers in the sample drawn from the 1911 census.

Not unlike the onion sellers, the two samples spanned the decades from young to old: the oldest clothes dealer was aged 75 years, and the youngest was aged 14 years. However, there is more consistency in the age distribution of the clothes dealers with significant numbers of prime working age: 63 per cent of the 1901 sample fall between the ages of 21 and 60 years, and 70 per cent of the 1911 sample fall into that same age group. Those under 21 years comprised 22 per cent and 18 per cent of the 1901 and 1911 samples respectively; similarly, low numbers were aged over 60 years, with only 15 per cent and 12 per cent falling into that group in the 1901 and 1911 samples respectively. Onion sellers were more likely to be very young, and their distribution across age groups is more scattered, an indication that selling clothes was, perhaps, a more permanent and stable source of subsistence income and employment for women across age groups. The clothes dealers in both cohorts were much more likely to be literate than the onion sellers, and the clothes dealers of 1911 were more likely to be literate than their peers in 1901: 56 per cent of the 1901 sample had basic literacy skills, and that number increased to 70 per cent in 1911.

Like the onion sellers, the clothes dealers were likely to be living in housing classified as 'second class'. Unlike the onion sellers, however, they were not always tenement dwellers: typically, the clothes dealer was more likely to be living in a private house, over a shop, or in a flat in a private house divided into flats. Despite variations in demographics, it is clear that the women who comprise the three cohorts were drawn from the working poor of Cork's city centre. Those living in a residence classified as second class was 73 per cent in the 1901 sample, and this was reduced slightly in 1911 to 70 percent. Of the 1901 sample, 27 per cent lived in a residence classified as 'first class', and this number rose slightly to 30 per cent of the 1911 sample. The data also suggests that a clothes dealer's contribution to the family economy meant that their earnings had the potential to help some to move above precarious living standards. The following narrative provides a closer look at the home lives of the clothes dealers who lived in the DED of medieval Cork City and who appeared in the census of 1901, and the census of 1911.

Several women were part of families that appeared positioned to transcend the precarious economic circumstances apparent in the lives of many of their peers. In 1901, Margaret Murphy, 60, was the head of a household shared with her working adult children. Her daughter Helena, 22, was also a clothes dealer. Margaret also had a daughter who was a dressmaker, one who was a milliner, and a son who was a frame maker. She was supporting her 12-year-old nephew who was in school. They lived in four rooms over a shop off the upscale Grand Parade. In 1911, Margaret Carroll, 63, was married to a tinplate worker. Their son, 26, was an undergraduate. They lived in five rooms. Catherine Rice, 42, was married to a harness merchant, and they operated a lodging house. They resided with their two children, aged 14 and 11 years and still in school. They had 11 lodgers. All lived in the 16 rooms of a private dwelling. For at least one family, clothes dealing appeared to be sustainable across generations and both censuses. In 1901, Mary Ellen Stark was married to a plumber; they had four children attending school, and one child aged six months. Mary Ellen's widowed mother, Eliza O'Neill, 64, was also a clothes dealer and lived with them. In 1911, Mary Ellen Stark, 45, was still married but her husband was now a waterworks superintendent. They lived with five of their children, the eldest of whom was working: Eliza, 22, was her mother's assistant. Eliza O'Neill, 74, Mary's widowed mother, was still living with them and she was still selling clothes. They lived in six rooms.

Stories such as theirs are, however, the exception. For widows with or without dependents, selling clothes was a vital source of income. In 1901, Bridget Coleman, 35, was a widow raising three children, aged 13, 10 and 8 years, all attending school. They lived in two rooms. Bridget was illiterate. In the 1911 census, Bridget Coleman, 45, was living with her son, daughter, son-in-law and two grandchildren. Her son-in-law was a labourer, her son was a butcher's porter, and her daughter was not working outside the home. They lived in three rooms. Also among the widows raising children in 1901 was Bridget O'Callaghan, 43; her daughter Mary, 28, was also a clothes dealer. Her son, 18, was a grocer's porter. Bridget was also raising three children who were enrolled in school. They lived in five rooms. Margaret Browne, 44, was also raising children; her son, 29 years, was a labourer; her 14-year-old daughter was in school. They lived in one room. Margaret Curtin, 43, was raising four children aged 10 years and under; her school-aged children were attending school. They lived in two rooms. Margaret Howard, a widow at 30 years, was raising two daughters, a 10-year-old and a toddler; the 10-year-old was attending school. They lived in a two-roomed house. In the 1911 census, Mary Foley, 45, was widowed and raising her 9-year-old daughter. They lived in one room. Likewise, Jane McCarthy, 31, was widowed and raising her nine-year-old son. They also lived in one room. Julia Sullivan, 45, was widowed and raising a 6-year-old son. They, too, lived in one room. Kate Sullivan, 46, was widowed; she and her daughter Ellie, 17, both sold clothes. They lived in three rooms.

In 1901, there were also widows contributing to a larger family economy. Mary Murphy, 60, was literate; however, her two daughters who were also clothes dealers, Hannah, 20, and Lizzie, 17, were recorded as illiterate. She also had a 15-year-old son who was an unemployed messenger. These four people lived in two rooms. Mary O'Leary, 66, was living with her son, a store clerk, and had taken in a boarder who was a labourer. They lived in a three-roomed house. Mary Hall, 65, lived with her daughter, 32, who was a domestic. They lived in one room.

The sale of clothes on the streets or in the markets also provided a means of support for widows supporting themselves. In 1901, Sara Mullaney, 50, was, like

Mary Gready, 44, widowed and living alone in two rooms. Mary Murphy was 50 and a widow in 1901, and living in one room. Likewise, Hannah O'Brien, 62, and Margaret Ryan, 60, were widows, and each was living alone in one room. In 1901, Hannah Donovan, 63, was living in a flat of two rooms and, in 1911, aged 75, she was still selling clothes and living alone in two rooms.

Clothes dealers also supported widows and other dependents, or contributed to the family economy of a home where a widow was the head of household. In 1901, Annie Carey, 21, was living with her widowed mother and two sisters, both of whom were working. They had also taken in two lodgers. These six people lived in 5 rooms. In 1901, Elizabeth Anne Downey, 21, and Catherine Downey, 16, were living with their widowed mother who was a shopkeeper, their brother who was a tinsmith, and a younger brother who was still in school. All were literate and lived in a six-roomed house. In 1911, Kate Woods, 26, sold clothes to support herself, her 76-year-old widowed aunt and a 76-year-old female lodger. They lived in two rooms. Hanna O'Brien, 18, was helping to support her widowed mother, along with her 15-year-old brother who worked in a factory; they had two younger siblings still in school. These five people lived in two rooms. Mary Buckley, 44, was supporting her widowed mother and her 29-year-old sister. They lived in four rooms.

Several of the clothes dealers had daughters who had taken up the trade, indicating that the sale of clothing may have been a sustainable enterprise for a woman when other opportunities to earn were rare. In 1901, Ellen Kettle, 51, was married to a labourer. Their daughter Ellen, 28, was also a clothes dealer. They lived in five rooms. Similarly, Julia Hegarty, 36, was married to a labourer; she and her daughter Julia, 17, were contributing to the family economy as clothes dealers. Mary Murphy, 40, was married to a blacksmith; their daughters, Nora, 17, and Margaret, 15, had also entered the trade. These five people lived in two rooms. Helena Mintern, 58, was married to a fisherman. Their daughter Nora, 27, was also in the trade, but her two adult sisters were housekeepers. Julia O'Mahoney, 58 and widowed, was living with her two daughters, Agnes 20, and Mary 19, both clothes dealers. The number of rooms they lived in was not recorded in the census data. In 1911, Kate Caulfield, 47, was married to a dock labourer. They had four children, two of whom were also clothes dealers: Mary, 18, and Kate, 14. The two youngest, both boys, were in school. These six people lived in three rooms.

The stories of these families illustrate that the sale of clothing bolstered the family finances primarily earned by labouring men. In addition to the aforementioned women who were married to labourers, in 1901 Hanoria Murray, 75, was a clothes dealer married to a clothes dealer. They lived in four rooms with their widowed daughter, 48, who was a housekeeper, and their 21-year-old grandson who was a tailor. Agnes O'Connell, 29, was married to a labourer. They had two children in school; they lived in two rooms. Nora Walsh, 40, was married to a cork maker. Their 15-year-old son was employed as a boot maker, and they had a younger son in school. These four people lived in one room. Mary Hayes, 18, was not married; her father was a labourer and her mother wasn't working. She had two brothers working as porters in shops, and a younger brother who was in school. These six people lived in two rooms.

Similar financial needs among families of the working poor were evident in the 1911 census. Ellen Webb, 24, was living with her father, a 60-year-old blacksmith and a widower. She was also living with three siblings; one, a sister, was unemployed. These five people lived in three rooms. Mary Ellen Quilligan, 17, lived with her parents and four siblings all under the age of 13; her father's sister-in-law and her young daughter also lived with them. She and her father, a chimney sweep, were the only members of the household who were working. Julia Mahoney, 24, resided with her mother, stepfather, and two brothers. Julia's mother did not work outside the home; her stepfather and two brothers were carpenters. Annie Riordan, 21, lived with her father, a dock labourer, and her mother, also a dealer, but what she sold was not specified. Her younger brother was a tailor's apprentice, her younger sister a housekeeper. They lived in four rooms.

The sale of clothes also assisted financially at the start of a married couple's life together. In 1901, Bridget Downing, 29, was married to a clothes dealer. They shared two rooms. Mary Duggan, 23, was married to a labourer; they had a daughter aged one. They lived with Mary's mother, a housekeeper, and Mary's younger sister. All were illiterate. They lived in three rooms. In 1911, Ellie McCarthy, 23, was married to a dock labourer. They shared two rooms. Hannah McCarthy, 34, was married to a bread truck driver. They were supporting two children aged five years and eight months. They lived in four rooms. Mary Fulignati, 29, was married to a 35-year-old cabinet maker from Italy. They had two sons aged four and three. They shared their home with a female domestic. These five people lived in three rooms. Mary Sheppard, 62, was married to a tinsmith. They lived with three adult children: two sons were employed as tinsmiths, the daughter was unemployed. These five people lived in three rooms.

Trading clothes was also the domain of women who were married but did not have a spouse in the home. In 1901, Annie Leahy, 48, was married and head of household. Her 18-year-old son was a porter in a shop; Annie had four children aged between four and 12 years. They lived in two rooms. Another Annie Leahy, 46, was head of household on the night of the 1911 census. Her daughter Annie McCarthy, 22, lived with her and also sold clothes; she was married but not living with her spouse. They also lived with Annie Leahy's 30-year-old stepson, a labourer and army reservist. Annie's 13-year-old son and her daughter, 17, were unemployed. These five people lived in three rooms. Eliza Hart, 30, was married but her spouse did not live with her; she was supporting a one-month-old daughter. She lived with her brother, a general labourer, a sister employed as a hairdresser, and a sister employed as a domestic. Margaret Mahoney, 22, lived with her father, a quay labourer, her mother, and nine siblings. Only Margaret, her father, and her 20-year-old brother, a soap factory hand, were employed. These twelve people lived in two rooms. Ellen O'Connell, 30, was married but her spouse was not in the home. She was supporting five children aged 10 years to 10 months. They lived in two rooms.

Single women supported themselves, and sometimes others in a family economy through the sale of clothes. Hester Hearde, 62, was single in 1901, and lived in a three-roomed house with her niece, also single, a 20-year-old seamstress. Bridget Harris, 40, was a widow who boarded with a baker, the baker's wife, and their three children. The number of rooms in their home was not indicated on the census. In 1911, Mary Twohig, 55, was single; she was the head of a household that included a 19-year-old niece, a tobacco spinner, and a 21-year-old nephew, a labourer. They lived in one room. Mary Ellen Sullivan, 18, lived with her father, mother, an older brother and a younger brother. Only Mary Ellen and her father, a labourer, were employed. These five people lived in three rooms.

William Bulfin, the travel writer who visited the Coal Quay during this era, provided an account of his close encounter with the Shawlies in 1907 that helps to round out these narratives. He described the traders in this street market as exclusively women, one he describes as 'cross-shawled'. Many were seen knitting while they worked, and chanting 'the praises of their socks and cradles and onions and fruit'. He provides an extensive list of what was sold there, including necessities of life that were affordable here for poor consumers: books and furniture, all second-hand, new and old clothes, fruit, vegetables, baskets, cradles, pans and tinware, stockings, sweets, cakes, lace, rosaries, and pictures. He further characterized the quality of many of their goods as 'hopeless case'. Of the Shawlies themselves, Bulfin wrote, 'there was no unkindliness in any of them'. 'Still', he added, 'I would be very slow to provoke them'.[19]

THE ARRIVAL OF TOWN PLANNING, GENTRIFICATION, AND THE 'SMALLER MEN'

This narrative of the Shawlies, along with Bulfin's account, calls into question the seemingly neutral nature of gentrification and its impact: calls to 'modernise' the medieval city centre by eliminating disorder from the streets and the footpaths, in addition to clearing the tenements in favour of macroeconomic interests, meant eliminating the primary source of income for the Shawlies. At the turn of the 20th century, the annual income of the Grand Parade Market was nearly double that of St Peter's and the Bazaar combined, and street trading often took the blame.[20] On 6 July 1910, the Corporation resolved to deal with the issue of vacant stalls in St Peter's and the Bazaar. However, rather than lower the rents to bring in traders from the streets, the Corporation prepared a scheme that would divide the market in two. In one half, the stalls that were tenanted would remain, with the remaining space to be leased to private interests.[21]

The first tenant appeared six years later. On 18 April 1916, Lord Mayor Thomas Butterfield announced that the government of Great Britain had allocated a munitions factory to Cork. After meeting with representatives of the military and the Minister for Munitions, various locations in the city were considered, but St Peter's was approved. The lord mayor stressed the urgency of handing over St Peter's, and invited representatives of the Trade and Labour Councils to give their views, but did not consult the stallholders. The proposal passed unanimously.[22] Provision was to be made in the Bazaar market for the displaced stallholders. After the war ended in 1918, St Peter's continued to be leased to private interests and never resumed life as a market, negating this 'indoor' option for women trading on the street, and leaving the displaced stallholders at a disadvantage. If the neighbourhood and markets were ignored or neglected by the local authority, the local business magnates of the city's firm-based economy were also happy to look the other way. In 1918, the vision that large, amalgamated business interests held of Cork as an economic centre commenced with great fanfare.

A series of public lectures on what were viewed as Cork's housing and town planning problems were given that year by D.J. Coakley, principal of the Cork Municipal School of Commerce, Joseph Delaney, the city engineer, and John J. Horgan, a solicitor with a distinct interest in town planning and municipal governance. Out of these lectures emerged *Cork – its trade and commerce 1918*, a pamphlet published by the Cork Incorporated Chamber of Commerce and Shipping (CICCS). It promoted the industrial, trading and shipping advantages of Cork to secure business and commercial interests in a planning document that favoured uses over citizens. Despite the plight and magnitude of Cork's urban poor being common knowledge, the CICCS wrote that the city was now at its most promising. Their vision for the future of Cork had nothing to offer the micro-economy, the poor or women. The working classes made a brief appearance in the mention of the Corporation's expenditure on over 60,000 working-class dwellings across the city. Labouring men in Cork were extolled, simply, as an industrial advantage. The poor were hinted at in a one-sentence entry under the heading 'Poor Law' in the description of the local authority. Women do not exist in the document's overview of the city's history, its population and its workforce. Its membership list reveals that women were not members. Of further significance is the limited voice of the working-class neighbourhood that had once been the city's centre. Approximately 60 full and half-page advertisements appear in the guide; only two were from businesses located on North Main Street, and only one from a business on Corn Market Street appeared. Of the organization's 251 members, those listed on North Main Street, South Main Street, and Corn Market Street totaled six, approximately 3 per cent of the membership.

As the 20th century advanced, the business interests that shaped the social, political and economic life of Cork had remained with rich and powerful men who continued to speak with a collective voice. However, there were shifts within that cohort: the emphasis was now on larger business interests, but not one centred solely on the 'merchant princes'. Their dominance in political life was in decline, and now power was increasing among new and growing commercial interests. This male-dominated sector was labelled by one observer as the 'smaller men': small grocers, victuallers and vintners who, having become as powerful as their wealthier forefathers, now turned their attention to political life in Cork, and formed associations to monitor the work of the merchant-dominated local authority.[23] One family of grocers with a story of growth during this era that aligns with the conceptualization of the 'smaller men' were also the one exception to the apparent 'absence' of businesses located in the medieval city centre in the CICCS business plans. They were the Musgrave Brothers Ltd with warehouses located on Corn Market Street.

Who were the Musgraves? According to the company's authorized history, two brothers, Thomas and Stuart Musgrave, rose to prominence from humble beginnings at 103 North Main Street, just north of St Peter's Market, where they opened a grocery in 1876. Eleven years later, in 1887, they opened a second shop on the more prestigious Grand Parade. At that stage, the brothers had accumulated over £10,000 in capital. Seven years on they formed Musgrave Brothers as a limited partnership. By 1894, they had left North Main Street and opened extensive and luxurious premises at 84 Grand Parade, next to the equally luxurious Queen's Old Castle department store at Grand Parade and Daunt's Square. In 1899, Musgrave Brothers recorded profits of £67,000. With the opening of the Corn Market Street premises, they had become wholesale suppliers to grocers of both commodities and store fixtures. During the years of the Great War, the Musgraves doubled their net profits resulting in remarkable growth for the company. On 30 December 1919, the Annual General Meeting of Musgrave Brothers Ltd was held. In the course of the meeting, a sum of £50,000 was approved by the shareholders for the purchase of additional buildings on Corn Market Street to house Ireland's first grocery wholesaler.[24]

The trade directories for Cork, *Guy's City and County Almanac and Directory,* from 1917 through 1919 show that the premises at nos 17–24 were held by small dealers including vintners, a furniture dealer, fish and provision stores, grocers and refreshment rooms. In 1922, the year that Ireland gained independence, Musgrave Brothers Ltd secured an overdraft totalling £19,200 with the Bank of Ireland using company shares as collateral.[25] According to the trade directory, Musgrave Brothers Ltd now controlled the premises from nos 17 to 24 on Corn Market Street. However, the company history reports that further progress on the facility was delayed due to the political situation in the country at the time. The political situation in Ireland, compounded by the increase in power of vested business interests after independence, would also present great challenges for women street traders. These were, however, the conditions that the Musgrave Brothers Ltd likely needed to secure their hold on Corn Market

Street, and continue with their plans for corporate expansion in the medieval city centre.

If the power of the merchants over the decisions of the local authority in Cork was clear from the 18th century onwards, the power of the interests of the 'smaller men' would later come to dominate those same decisions. This was the case with decisions that shaped the two neighbourhoods in the city's centre. Both were clearly defined by class, and both were gendered: the Shawlies dominated the more precarious trade of food and used clothing on the streets of the medieval city centre. They were able to trade close to the city centre, but only if they were 'contained' outside of Cork's privileged retail and commercial core. The data gathered on these girls and women who sold onions and clothing on the streets confirms what was known about the Shawlies from the sparse accounts that were available: they struggled economically, and street trading was the means by which hundreds of women earned a subsistence living on the streets. The 'modern' vision that created St Patrick's Street continued to dominate into the 20th century as the power in Cork shifted to the 'smaller men' who influenced local governance. This shift meant that this same vision was transposed onto the wider economic plans for the city and its corresponding gentrification, much to the exclusion of those in the margins.

2. 'A very distinct interest in having order kept in the street': the sway of the 'smaller men'

It seems peculiar that, in the aftermath of both the Anglo-Irish War and the Irish Civil War, the Irish Free State would choose to focus its efforts on a comprehensive programme to regulate street trading; however, that is how the story unfolds. The uncertain economic and political circumstances, conditions that continue to push women into street trading to this day, were not only present but were exacerbated through many of the economic and social policies pursued by those who formed the Irish Free State government. At the same time, vested interests were trying to have street trading banned. The government was also responsible for the dissolution of the local authorities in both Dublin and Cork, replacing them with commissioners who used their unchecked powers to respond to the calls for outright bans. The debates of Dáil Éireann back to 1919 reveal that, prior to 1924, there were no references to street trading, with the exception of truancy concerns and children trading on the streets rather than attending school. The same is true of the newspaper coverage of the issue: a review of the database of the *Irish Times* produces very few references to street trading excepting those concerned with truancy. When statements about street trading as a public blight, originating with those who held social and economic power, begin to appear in the press, the power of a negative discourse to demonize these women is very clear.

While the story told in this book is that of Cork's Shawlies, the impetus for the Act came from the centre of power in Dublin, and spread to the streets of Cork. On 6 October 1921, an article appeared in the *Irish Times* that characterized street trading as 'evil'. The correspondent described a meeting of the executive committee of a group that called itself the Dublin Citizens' Association (DCA). Despite the name's emphasis on citizenship, the DCA was, according to the article, comprised of 'substantial ratepayers' from 'incorporated firms' exercising their right to 'criticise and investigate any rate or any action of the Corporation that they thought should be questioned'. The DCA declared that the growth of street trading was compromising 'the common law rights of the citizens', and presented 'specific unfairness to the taxpaying traders'. Street trading, the article continued, was contributing to the unsanitary conditions in Dublin's streets. The next reference to street trading in the *Irish Times* did not appear until 4 June 1923; it was an opinion-editorial piece entitled 'Street trading in Dublin', subtitled 'A nuisance and a blot on the city'. On 5 October 1923, a letter to the editor appeared that blamed traders for chaos and the loss of business. The letter was signed 'Disgusted'.

In Cork, a marked shift in the nature and volume of the complaints against the Shawlies began in 1922, coinciding with the complaints instigated in Dublin by the DCA. The notion that street trading posed a threat to public health and safety, and that it represented a threat to ratepayers, including 'bricks and mortar' traders, intensified in the discourse surrounding a ban in Cork just as it had in Dublin.

THE PUBLIC RECORD

A campaign began at the HCC meeting on 21 March 1922 when a letter from a group called the Cork Traders' Protective Association (CTPA) was read. They alleged that interference to businesses was caused by obstructed footpaths on North Main Street and also on Castle Street.[1] In the council minutes of 22 September, a letter from the CTPA was read alleging 'serious injury' to the shopkeepers in North Main Street and Castle Street by street traders. An immediate ban was requested. The matter was referred back to the HCC.[2] On 17 October, the letter was read at the HCC meeting, and the street inspector was told to prohibit street traders from placing their wares on the footpaths in selected streets.[3] The efforts by the CTPA resumed at the council meeting on 27 November. A letter from William Mockler, the group's solicitor, was read that painted an extreme picture of the situation in North Main Street. Street traders were accused of seriously interfering with the business of shopkeepers. The CTPA referred to other cities that protected the trading of shopkeepers and asked that the same be done in Cork. Despite the severity of the situation as depicted in Mockler's letter, the complaint was simply referred to the HCC.[4]

On 16 January 1923, the HCC heard letters from several unnamed businesses in North Main Street that referenced the obstructions complained of previously. These letters were considered by the HCC along with complaints of obstructions made outside the premises of large firms; this factor makes it difficult to determine if the obstructions referred to here were, in fact, made by the firms themselves or by street traders. A special meeting was called to address street obstructions as a whole. That meeting took place on 23 January. Again, no action was taken. At the HCC meeting on 20 March, a councillor drew attention to an obstruction created by stalls on the footpath in Daunt's Square. This was also referred to the street inspector.[5]

On 27 April, the council minutes recorded that another letter from Mockler on behalf of the CTPA was read, complaining of persistent obstructions in North Main Street and in Castle Street. The complaints named Daunt's Square and Princes Street off St Patrick's Street. These obstructions were categorized as a threat to shopkeepers, and the CTPA threatened legal action if the obstructions continued. The target of that threat was not specified in the minutes.[6] That meeting was covered in the *Cork Examiner* and yet, despite the scope and volume of the complaint, there was no coverage of this portion of the meeting. The matter was referred to the HCC again, and the letter was read at the HCC meeting on 15 May. Despite the repetition of the complaint and the threat of legal action, the complaint was simply referred to the street inspector. A report of that meeting was read at council on 8 June 1923 but there was no discussion on the matter. There would be no further discussions on the matter of street trading for more than a year.

'SMALLER MEN'

Larger events impacting the governance of Cork in the years 1923 and 1924 would, however, prove significant in the trading lives of the Shawlies, although the players and their roles in the governance of the city seem very far removed. It is at this juncture that John J. Horgan, one of the instigators of the town-planning ethos in Cork in 1918, moved to the fore. In 1923, he founded the Cork Progressive Association (CPA) to lobby for an American-style or 'business model' of municipal management to be implemented in Cork. The membership of the CPA was drawn largely from the city's Chamber of Commerce and the CICCS. The CPA conflated 'progressive' with the protection and promotion of commercial interests and the macro-economy, and a cost-effective local authority that privileged that economy. Not unlike the DCA in Dublin, citizenship and the voice that comes with it was equated with 'ratepayer'. Furthermore, this group was not politically neutral, having entered an 'election pact' with the Cumann na nGaedheal government of William T. Cosgrave.[7]

According to correspondence that originated with the CPA in 1923, their goal was to protect the interests of taxpayers and ratepayers while securing representation for business interests in public bodies including the Oireachtas. According to a letter soliciting memberships, the CPA was expressly concerned with the potential outcomes of upcoming national and local elections. They believed there existed 'a grave danger' that 'the interests of the commercial and industrial classes' would be 'seriously imperilled' unless 'looked after with energy and promptitude'.[8] In December 1923, the CPA called upon the Department of Local Government and Public Health to hold an inquiry under the Local Government (Temporary Provisions) Act, 1923, into what they alleged were wasteful practices in the administration of the local authority's business.[9] The arrogance of the CPA and Horgan, believing that they knew what was best for the general populous, is encapsulated in a letter to the editor of the *Cork Examiner* dated 11 October 1924. The author cites a lecture given by Horgan that had appeared in the *Examiner* a few days earlier where Horgan claimed that the 'ignorance of the electors' had prompted his call for the Corporation's dissolution, and a need for 'democratic autocracy'.

Then, in April 1924, at the Annual General Meeting of Musgrave Brothers Ltd it was announced that construction on the Corn Market Street facility would begin. The company hoped to have it completed by the end of the year.[10] On 9 July 1924, complaints against street traders resumed. At a meeting of the Law and Finance Committee, a councillor raised the matter of the obstruction on Corn Market Street by the sale of vegetables, and suggested that indoor space be provided for street traders in the Corn Market building on Angelsea Street. The matter was then referred to the HCC to have the obstruction by-laws enforced.[11] In the minutes of the HCC meeting on 15 July 1924, this plan was mentioned – but not in detail, and consideration was deferred. There would be no further action on this suggestion to relocate the Shawlies. Complaints about street trading are absent from the public record until August 1924 when the inquiry into the administrative affairs of the Corporation commenced.

Although the inquiry was to deal with larger allegations of corruption, nepotism and ineptitude on the part of the Corporation, street trading was used to illustrate the alleged ineffectiveness of the local authority. On 6 September 1924, the *Irish Times* ran an article briefly detailing concerns about street trading that were voiced at the inquiry. The newspaper reported that the CTPA had told the inquiry of hazards and obstructions caused by street traders, and the failure of the Corporation to address the problem. They alleged that a line of stalls measuring 150 yards lined North Main Street. These echoed the complaints submitted to council earlier, and included the earlier allegations that Castle Street, Daunt's Square and Princes Street were obstructed by street traders. Now, however, Corn Market Street, where the Musgrave Brothers' wholesale facility was planned, appeared on the list of streets where street trading was now a nuisance and a hazard.

On Tuesday 16 September 1924, the Street Inspector provided the HCC with a list of both street traders and shopkeepers causing obstructions in North Main Street and Washington Street. At that same meeting a solicitor spoke on behalf of street traders in North Main Street. He told the HCC that the street traders would experience a significant hardship, and would be 'deprived of their livelihood' if action were taken against them. He advised that many were forced to trade in the street because the continued lease of St Peter's Market to private interests had meant they lost their stalls there.[12] According to a report in the *Cork Examiner*, their solicitor noted that some of the displaced traders had been trading for decades, and had not been permitted to resume trading in St Peter's after the munitions factory closed. Furthermore, he estimated a ban on street trading would push hundreds into poverty because they supported relatives and family. He asked the Corporation to create a market for them. After a discussion, the HCC felt an alternative should be found that would allow those trading on the street to continue trading and earning. Lord Mayor Sean French was in attendance. He suggested a special meeting of the HCC be scheduled to consider the question of street trading on the whole. In the interim, he advised, no action would be taken.[13]

That meeting took place on 23 September 1924. On the same day, a letter to the editor of the *Cork Examiner,* signed 'Citizen', appeared in the newspaper. Written from a position of support for women street traders, the tone is distinctly sarcastic and as such the characterization of the Shawlies is derogatory. It opened by highlighting the abuse the women had suffered by ill-informed people. The author reiterated many of the earlier complaints regarding hygiene, odours, danger and economic threats to shops, proposed that disease-addled goods were needed to foster immunity across the population, and suggested the extension of street trading to St Patrick's Street, the South Mall, and the Grand Parade. As for protecting the interests of 'bricks and mortar' traders referred to as 'bloated profiteers', the author asked why 'poor, downtrodden street traders, with large, helpless families' and husbands who choose not to work, be required to 'pay rents for market stalls' rather than be removed from the streets.

When the special meeting of the HCC meeting took place on 23 September, William Mockler, the solicitor who had represented the CTPA, was in attendance but was now representing Musgrave Brothers Ltd. The firm now moved to the fore in this issue, and allowed Musgraves, through their representative, to articulate both 'legitimate' trade and 'legitimate' uses of public space. The account in the minutes of Mockler's appearance on 23 September 1924 before the HCC is very brief. He told the HCC that Musgraves had recently built an extensive facility on the east side of Corn Market Street at a cost of £20,000. In light of this sum, Mockler requested that street trading be confined to the west side of Corn Market Street. He then said that the street traders were interfering with what he termed 'legitimate trading' conducted by Musgraves who, he added, were significant ratepayers, invoking the privilege that comes with that status. He then asked that steps be taken to end street trading in Daunt's Square, and offered his legal firm's assistance to the Corporation to help the situation.[14]

A more detailed picture was provided in the *Cork Examiner.* In this account, discussion of the issue started with Councillor Gamble, the elected representative for the Corn Market Street area. He reminded the HCC that two markets, St Peter's and the Bazaar, had previously been available for petty traders. He reminded the committee St Peter's continued to be leased by private interests with influence. Councillor Gamble then acknowledged a deputation representing Musgraves, and asked if they should be present during the discussion as they were not on the agenda. He insisted that the HCC was compelled to follow the agenda. The account then described a dispute among the committee's members over the presence of Mockler and his right to address the meeting. The chair, Councillor M.J. O'Riordan, advised: 'We are here as public representatives attending a public meeting, and the public are entitled to come here and state their grievances'. Gamble then observed that Cork's poor

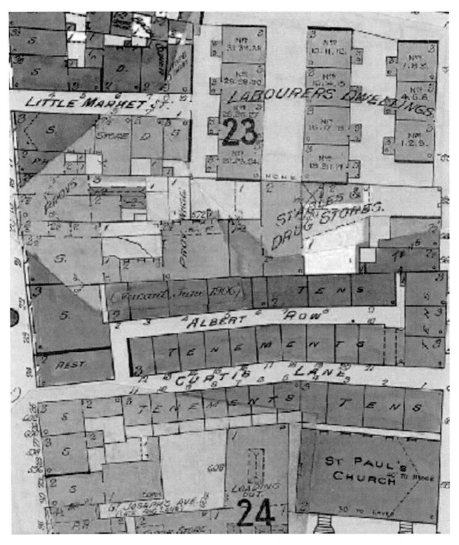

2. Goad Plan 1909

were not part of this 'public' meeting. Sean French intervened and asked for Mockler's assistance in the matter because he felt that Musgraves had a valid objection: street traders on the footpath were not conducive to business. He then cautioned that an immediate ban would inflict financial hardship on these women. French then expressed concern that the situation would only become worse, but added that the HCC should provide for an alternative to allow the traders to continue to earn.

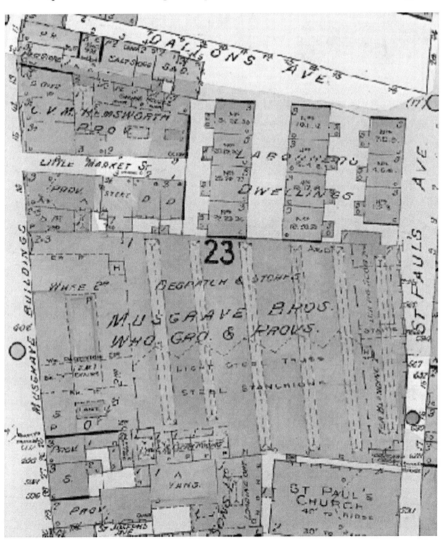

3. Goad Plan 1938

Mockler proceeded amid Gamble's protest, beginning a lengthy address with the observation that French's opinion aligned with that of his clients. The building on Corn Market Street, he observed, would house a 'large retail trade', and so Musgraves 'had a very distinct interest in having order kept in the street'. He asked that street trading be permitted on one-third of the west side of Corn Market Street, reserving the middle of the road and the east side for propertied businesses. He said this was enough, and the street traders would be able to maintain their custom. His complaint then shifted from Corn Market Street to adjoining streets where, Mockler implied, street trading was disruptive as it interfered with people accessing the warehouse from St Patrick's Street. He insisted that street trading on Castle Street be prohibited. His attention then turned to Daunt's Square, where he said that 'onion sellers' were obstructing the footpath, and that he believed the HCC would agree that proper access to Corn Market Street was necessary. He added that Musgraves were pleased the Corporation had called this special meeting on the issue, and they believed that regulations must be made and enforced. He concluded with an additional rationale for administrative action: street trading results in litter, which made it 'very hard on people paying high rates to carry on business' in what he termed 'the ordinary way'.

According to the newspaper account, Councillor Gamble then reminded the HCC that at previous meetings the objections had been to street trading in North Main Street but now, he observed, Corn Market Street had become the focus. Gamble then observed that Musgraves' facility on Corn Market Street was a wholesale business, and said he could not understand how the street traders posed a threat. Gamble then highlighted the threat to the Shawlies posed by this proposition, because of their economic vulnerability. He observed that the HCC had been persistent in trying to get street traders to move from Daunt's Square to the end of Corn Market Street; they were now asked to eliminate them altogether. He said he sympathized because the company was creating employment, but he could not support measures that were injurious to the poor. According to this account the meeting was then adjourned.[15]

When it did resume on 25 September 1924, a solicitor appeared on behalf of street traders in Corn Market Street, another represented those in Daunt's Square, and Mockler returned on behalf of Musgraves. However, according to the minutes there was just a discussion on a proposition made by the lord mayor. It was agreed unanimously that street trading would be restricted to the west side of Corn Market Street. The street inspector was authorized to prosecute anyone found obstructing the east side of Corn Market Street. For the first time, the idea of licensing street traders was announced. These would be issued at a nominal fee in order to have 'control over the present traders', and no new licenses would be issued 'for a period to be specified'. A rationale was not provided. As for the Shawlies trading outside the Princes Street Market, accommodation was to be found for them inside the English Market.[16] On 7 October 1924, at a meeting of the TMC, Lord Mayor French picked up the cause of the Shawlies: he asked that estimates be made for the cost of building an open shelter on Lavitt's Quay for the sale of produce. This motion was seconded by Councillor Hennessy and passed.[17] However, this and his earlier recommendation for accommodation to be found within the Princes Street Market for the Shawlies would end here. On 30 October, the verdict following the inquiry into the administration of the Cork Corporation was released: Seamus Burke, the Minister for Local Government and Public Health, dissolved the local authority in Cork.

On 31 October 1924, Philip Monahan delivered the order of dissolution to a meeting of the council in Cork. The former mayor of Drogheda, and more recently the county commissioner in Kerry, Monahan was appointed the city commissioner for Cork by Minister Seamus Burke, and took up the post on 11 November 1924. On 10 November 1924, the *Cork Examiner* printed a very detailed protest by Lord Mayor Sean French and members of the Corporation against the dissolution order. Details of each charge of neglect in governance were addressed with the details of actions the Corporation had taken. As for street trading, it was characterized as 'one of the most difficult problems with which the Corporation had been confronted' as 'many poor people' had for many years become accustomed to 'buying and selling in certain recognised places'. Street trading got a brief mention in the report of the Department's inspector who presided over the inquiry. He wrote that the TMC was ineffective in dealing with the issue. It is clear from the review of the HCC meeting that council had not made a decision to end street trading in the main, however his report indicates that council had decided to ban trading. Of that decision he wrote that 'Good intentions seldom benefit ratepayers'.[18]

DEMOCRATIC AUTOCRACY

Horgan and the CPA got their wish: as commissioner, Phillip Monahan was effectively the local authority in Cork, acting as the city's council, mayor and its committees. Thus, when a committee was meeting, Monahan heard reports and made decisions alone. What had been council meetings were now a 'special sitting' of the commissioner where, again, he made decisions alone. All were held in his office at Fitzgerald's Park, a municipal museum located west of the city's centre, and the location of the industrial exhibition that had opened the century. A review of the minutes of the TMC and HCC for the period when Monahan was commissioner indicate a 'bottom-line' style of cost administration. In administering the Corporation-owned markets, for example, contracts for repairs were given to the lowest bidder, and leases for stalls were given to the highest bidder. On 18 November 1924, Monahan presided for the first time over the TMC. The minutes record that the market inspector's report showed that, after looking for accommodation in the Princes Street Market for the Shawlies trading outside its entrance, he had found no accommodation there. Monahan ordered that they be removed from the street and the search for accommodation ceased.[19]

Monahan would have a unilateral hold on power until 1929, and it was only then that the Street Trading Act (1926) was implemented in Cork. There is no mention of the Act in the minutes of the HCC, TMC or in the minutes of

Monahan's solo sittings as commissioner. During that time the Street Trading Act (1926) had been passed into law by the Free State government. The Minister for Justice, Kevin O'Higgins, had insisted when he introduced the legislation that it was meant to create fairness in trading, and was not a ban.[20] In practice, however, the reality for Dublin's women street traders was very different. On one occasion during readings of the bill that would become the legislation, Bryan Cooper, TD, raised an amendment calling for the option of imprisonment on the first violation of the Act. His rationale, which he felt secure expressing publicly in Dáil Éireann, was that it would not be easy to collect the fines from street traders. He went on to characterize them as resembling 'fleas' that 'hop about from one street to another' and, when caught, 'it is difficult to get them to disgorge their ill-gotten gains'.[21] His observations were not objected to by Minister O'Higgins or other members of the Dáil.

Almost immediately following the passage into law of the Act early in 1927, concerns regarding persecution were raised in Dáil Éireann. Thomas Nagle, TD, first called for an inquiry in February and then again on 31 March. Amid a flurry of prosecutions, he alleged that many street traders were not aware of the law until they were charged. He also indicated that he and other deputies had tried to speak with Dublin's city commissioners to advocate for the street traders but were ignored. The Minister for Local Government and Public Health, Seamus Burke, remained firm: there would be no inquiry despite allegations of the Act being implemented without due process and input from the street traders.[22] The fact that Nagle and others had tried and did not gain access to the commissioners speaks to the limited voice of street traders, even when elected officials were representing them. It also demonstrates the degree to which civic commissioners were willing and able to wield unilateral power and shape the city of Dublin at will. Perhaps most telling, when he first prescribed streets in Dublin where street trading would be prohibited, O'Higgins confined the list to approximately 16 streets. Dublin's commissioners later expanded the list, unchecked, to approximately 250 streets according to the list published in the *Irish Times* on 27 January 1927.

Having largely ignored or sidelined the issue, in 1928, as Philip Monahan's term as commissioner was drawing to a close and the local authority was about to be reformed and re-established, he took it upon himself to bring the Street Trading Act to Cork. According to an article in the *Irish Times* on 23 June 1928, Monahan announced that he had opted to follow Dublin, and regulate street traders under powers that the 1926 Act gave him. He specified North Main Street, and said he would abolish street trading there out of necessity as vehicular traffic had become heavier. He characterized street trading as 'dangerous', noting it had resulted in several accidents. He then promised to find accommodation for the displaced street traders. There are no references to street trading in committee minutes, in the minutes of the special sitting of the commissioner, nor is there correspondence on the subject during this time in the by-law file. However, on 16 July 1928 the *Irish Times* reported on a period of 'grace' for Cork's street traders. The article indicates that the Street Trading Act, 1926, was operational in Cork, but would not be enforced until the end of the year. The article reported that representatives of street traders had met with Monahan, and had vowed to leave North Main Street before the deadline if they could continue to trade in the interim. Monahan was reported to have reluctantly agreed because he felt obliged to compromise.

It is clear that Monahan was using his unilateral power to regulate street trading, as the design and implementation of a law governing street trading in Cork was ambiguous. Evidently, Monahan found some comfort to do so and regulate the trading of the Shawlies without a solid challenge to stop him. That article, published in July, had reported that the Street Trading Act, 1926, was operative in Cork, and that Monahan was reluctant to offer a period of grace for the displacement of the traders. However, according to correspondence held at the Cork City and County Archives,[23] it was not until 7 August 1928 that Monahan wrote to the Dublin town clerk to request a copy of Dublin's by-laws governing street trading. Furthermore, on 23 August 1928, Cork's town clerk issued a notice to be published in the *Cork Examiner* and the *Evening Echo* indicating that the Act would take effect in Cork from 1 January 1929. However, it was not until 22 October that he wrote to both the Department of Local Government and Public Health, and the Department of Justice, to advise that Monahan had resolved to adopt the Act at the sitting of the commissioner in September. There is no account in Cork's official record of this resolution. On 7 November, the Department of Local Government and Public Health wrote and acknowledged that the Act would come into operation in Cork on 1 January 1929.

According to the minutes of a sitting of the commissioner on 9 November, this letter was read and Monahan stated that the Act would come into effect on 1 January 1929. In the interim, according to correspondence from An Garda Síochána in Cork dated 31 December 1928, Monahan ordered a registry be compiled of street traders, and this was carried out in October and November 1928. The criteria for registration was anyone exposing goods for sale in the city who could be called a 'street trader'. The chief superintendent noted that their numbers were significant, and that it was probable there would be new applicants for licences when the by-laws passed. He then added that he understood Monahan intended to limit licences to existing street traders. Without naming prohibited streets, he suggested that Monahan keep in mind the future of the city's centre. Using terms that invoked both a modern and a middle-class vision of Cork, he suggested that 'regard should be had to the necessity at some future date' to reserve 'certain wide streets for parking omnibuses and motor cars', adding that these same wide streets should not be allocated to 'street traders' and 'motor parks', the latter being what are now known as taxi ranks.

On the same day, the town clerk issued a notice that the commissioner would hold a special sitting on 4 January 1929. The minutes of that sitting indicate that a letter from the secretary to the Minister of Local Government and Public Health was read, and it advised that Monahan's proposed by-laws were approved. A list of prohibited streets was requested as soon as possible. The minutes note that the commissioner made a statement to the press about the intentions behind the by-laws, along with the locations where street trading was prohibited. There was no explanation as to the discrepancy between what was reported in July 1928 about street trading regulations in Cork, nor was this discrepancy reported on in the press coverage of the meeting. Only Monahan's statement to the press was covered in the *Cork Examiner* on 5 January. He announced that a prohibition would apply to all streets with certain exceptions. A number of other regulations were detailed, including hours for trading, and dimensions for stalls or pushcarts. Prohibitions were placed on cleaning fish and plucking fowl, vegetables carrying dirt or soil could not be exposed for sale; and stallholders had to carry a container for refuse.

Monahan insisted that the by-laws would not abolish street trading, but would regulate it to eliminate obstructions to both traffic and the business of 'bricks and mortar' traders. He said it was well known that the Act had been adopted, and the Corporation had the power to prohibit street trading in any street. He described street traders as a 'hard-working, decent body of people, who deserve a good deal of public sympathy' and insisted he was 'anxious to cause them as little trouble as possible'. He then continued to problematize them. He described conditions in North Main Street, Daunt's Square and the North Gate Bridge as intolerable. Street traders, he went on, obstructed traffic, and he expressed concern that both they and pedestrians were in danger when forced to walk on the roadway. He then issued the warning that Gardaí had the right to seize goods from traders working in prohibited streets.

The geographical limits he set indicate that he intended to formally contain the Shawlies in the working-class neighbourhood of the medieval city centre, but off footpaths in front of businesses. He allowed them to trade on Kyle Street and Corn Market Street, but only next to established street traders. They were permitted to trade on selected quays; however, they were only allowed to pitch in the limited space on the riverside. Trading was permitted on Lavitt's Quay, but only between Corn Market Street and Half-Moon Street, which kept the Shawlies from the approach to St Patrick's Street and landmarks such as the Opera House. They were permitted on the riverside of Pope's Quay, but only for 100 yards from a position 50 yards east of the North Gate Bridge. This would effectively contain the Shawlies on the approach to North Main Street. Monahan said those who vacated North Main Street, North Gate Bridge and Daunt's Square could pitch a stall in the authorized locations. If they did so, he added, it was 'likely' they would not meet with 'further interference'; if they did not, Monahan promised 'reluctantly' to 'make use of all the powers' provided by the Act. He threatened prosecution and fines if the regulations were not followed. He cautioned them to honour their undertaking in the grace period or, in the following month, face the consequences when the Act would be in full force.

A notice appeared in the *Cork Examiner* on 7 January 1929, and on 8 January the Cork town clerk wrote to the secretary to the Minister for Local Government and Public Health confirming the adoption of the Act. Street trading did not appear in the council minutes until 15 March 1929, Monahan's last sitting as commissioner. At that time he resolved, according to correspondence, that application be made to the Minister for the confirmation of the street trading by-laws made on 4 January 1929, and the changes made on 8 February 1929. Evidently, Monahan knew that the by-laws were not in place, and yet this did not prevent him from making statements and threats that prohibitions were in place and prosecutions were possible from July 1928 onwards. Furthermore, the minutes of 8 February do not mention street trading or stall trading.

The next piece of correspondence that appears in the by-law file held at the Cork City and County Archives indicates that, at Monahan's request, the Act was never properly applied in Cork. This information is revealed in copies of letters forwarded to Cork's town clerk on 1 July 1929. The first letter was sent on 14 June 1929 from the secretary to the Minister of Justice to the secretary to the Minister for Local Government and Public Health. The Minister of Justice had reported that Monahan 'now holds the view that it is not necessary at present to have the Act enforced' because his goal was to have 'street traders removed from three streets' considered unsuitable. As that goal had been met, Monahan was described as 'satisfied with the present position' and 'suggested that the matter should be allowed to rest'. The secretary concluded that, 'it would not appear to be necessary to take any further steps to bring the provisions of the Act into operation'. In the next letter, dated 1 July, the secretary to the Minister for Local Government and Public Health advised the secretary to the Minister for Justice that Minister Mulcahy would not proceed further with the by-laws. The Act would remain as such for nearly 10 more years.

The call to ban street trading started in Dublin and coincided with the politically and economically powerful individuals' plans to modernize the capital of the new Irish state. Street trading was problematized by those vested interests and the government responded, passing the Street Trading Act, 1926. The Shawlies were problematized in Cork soon thereafter. In both cities, regulations purporting to create 'fairness' in the marketplace were used to remove women street traders from the streets favoured by vested commercial interests. The implementation of these regulations was, clearly, facilitated by the dissolution of the Corporations in Dublin and Cork, thereby allowing commissioners appointed by the Free State government to use their unilateral powers to hyper-regulate street trading and ignore concerns expressed about the potential of these limits to further impoverish women street traders. In Cork, the Act was used as a threat of sorts by Philip Monahan to move the Shawlies off certain streets where business interests objected to them. He did not follow due process for an actual, enforceable prohibition, and he proceeded in this manner with the complicity of the Irish Free State government. Despite the appearance of some advocates on their behalf, the voices of Cork's Shawlies were muted in these discussions and decisions that governed their futures.

3. 'We're here nearly all our lives': documentation and displacement of the Shawlies

Despite their numbers, entrenched social relations and processes had pushed the Shawlies further into the margins of the local economy and society. Again, who were these women, and why was access to street trading so vital for them? Chapter 2 attempted to answer these questions, based on information in the 1901 and 1911 censuses. The 1928 registry,[1] and the information recorded by Gardaí, provides further information about their lives and reasons for trading on the eve of the introduction of the Street Trading Act, 1926. When Monahan ordered Gardaí to compile a registry of all the street traders in Cork, this was carried out in the city centre, and in a commercial district in a working-class neighbourhood on the city's north side.

All of the 199 traders listed in the registry were women. The registry lists their names, ages and addresses, and professional particulars such as commodities sold, length of time trading and location of their pitches. Only 14 were itinerant, an overwhelming majority were 'stall traders' that had traded from a fixed location established over time. Of the total number of women street traders, 161 or 81 per cent were trading in the city centre. In Cork, the new legislation worked in tandem with social processes entrenched in class and gender roles, expectations and privileges to facilitate the gradual disappearance of the Shawlies, and allowed for the abuse of their rights in the service of amalgamated business interests. At the same time, however, larger historical processes served as contingencies that created the need for women to be able to independently access the streets as marketplaces for survival.

As noted in the introduction, conditions such as an economic downturn putting men out of work, an economy that does not produce work for women, and displacement and instability due to warfare, continue to push women into street trading in the 21st century. According to one observer, those who were disenfranchised in Irish society early in the history of the state were those whose interests did not align with the interests of elites, or those 'who represented modes of living and ways of earning a living that were obsolescent', such as grocers and sweetshop proprietors, or were 'declared to be anti-social', such as working women.[2] Street traders were not listed, but they would have fallen lower on the social ladder than small grocers; they were definitely working women. Austerity measures and policy directives of the first Free State government in response to its lack of capital and the substantial reconstruction debt that followed the Anglo-Irish War and the Irish Civil War point to larger attacks on the poor and women. This context likely eased implementation of the Street Trading Act, 1926.

In response to the daunting expense of reconstructing the fledgling Irish state, William T. Cosgrave, as the government's acting Minister for Finance 1922–3, passed fiscal responsibility for reconstruction onto local authorities,[3] a move that likely created a need locally to raise revenues through fees and fines provided by regulations such as those in the Street Trading Act, 1926. After the cost of repairing infrastructure, one of the state's most significant expenditures was pensions. Ernest Blythe, the first Minister for Finance, made significant cuts to the old age pension in 1924 by limiting both the payout and the entitlement,[4] putting poor women at a particular disadvantage: 67,000 of the 114,000 of persons receiving the old age pension were women.[5] That same budget also carried a reduction in income tax equivalent to the decrease in the Old Age Pension, leading to widespread public allegations that Blythe favoured the wealthy in Irish society. The Minister for Local Government, Seamus Burke, justified the cut by citing 'one of the most serious defects of the Irish character' as 'dependence', indicating that an increased number of Irish citizens were leading 'a parasitic existence'.[6] Burke was the Minister for Local Government when the Street Trading Act, 1926, was created, and he confirmed the first by-laws submitted by the commissioners in Dublin.

Burke was not the only political leader in the government to express negative sentiments towards the poor. In October 1924, during a debate in Dáil Éireann about the crippling unemployment problem in the state, the Minister for Industry and Commerce, Patrick McGilligan, announced that 'people may have to die in this country and die of starvation'.[7] Later that year, the government eliminated unemployment insurance, only to reintroduce it with new legislation in 1926 when the unemployment rate was approximately 12 per cent. What were the implications for women street traders? This was the same era when working women were viewed, increasingly, as threats to employed men, and the state did not prioritize creating employment for women. Yet, unemployment among women previously employed in factories and trades was prevalent and further deepened by displacement following advances in mechanization.[8] The unemployment rate among domestics and those employed as agricultural labourers was significant, and in 1926, more than half of working Irish women were employed in those two sectors. Both sectors were also excluded from receiving unemployment insurance. While women may have been disproportionately affected by unemployment, in 1927, William T. Cosgrave would not appoint a woman to the Relief of Unemployment Committee, and its report released in 1928 did not even mention women.[9]

For the very poor, workhouses that had been available to the very destitute were closed and were replaced with relief payments, but these were available for only one month at a time. It was also highly stigmatized, and more women than men applied for themselves and their children; they included widows, deserted wives, and unmarried mothers.[10] Even married women who numbered among the poor and working classes may have needed to supplement the family income as men in the newly independent Ireland also encountered problems finding work, including many who lost work in the local authorities amid fiscal cutbacks in areas such as road work. Government employment schemes during this period paid very little. It is very likely, then, that these women and others, who were poor and disproportionately affected by the combined trends, would turn to street trading to survive.

THE SHAWLIES ARE DOCUMENTED

As noted earlier, of the total number of women street traders, 81 per cent were trading in the city centre, and it is these Shawlies for whom demographic profiles have been compiled from the information in the 1928 registry. Analysis of the impact of regulation that was likely, and the importance of trading in their lives, is guided by the rationales provided by Monahan for the need to regulate street trading, and that of critics calling for a ban.

Of the 147 women designated as stall traders, 40 per cent were selling old clothes, and 48 per cent were selling food, typically fruit and vegetables. It is likely their trade met the demands of poor and working-class consumers searching for affordable necessities. An additional 12 per cent sold miscellaneous items such as chandlery, wares and used books. The women trading on the street in the market district immediately surrounding St Peter's Market and the Bazaar numbered 47 per cent on Corn Market Street, 46 per cent on North Main Street, and another 5 per cent selling on Kyle Street which runs between the two thoroughfares. From these numbers it is clear that displacement of the traders on North Main Street, in conjunction with those displaced by the ban placed in front of Musgraves on the east side of Corn Market Street, would result in significant crowding on Corn Market Street. It is likely that this move would have a dramatic impact on their ability to earn due to increased competition and crowding. Monahan's concession of allowing these women to trade on the quays, but only on the river side, would also have put many of them out of easy reach of customers. The creation of more space in St Peter's Market was never discussed, and yet many of the women trading on the street had been displaced when space was leased to private interests.

The implementation of the Act, under these circumstances, would have significantly compromised the earning potential of all 144 women, both in terms of reducing available space, increased competition, and increased costs in the form of licensing fees. The frequency of trading is also significant: 124 (84 per cent) of respondents reported trading daily, an indication that this was full-time employment. Only 22 (15 per cent) reported trading on Saturdays only, and one woman traded only on Fridays and Saturdays. Thus, the vast majority of women were trading from an established location daily: this was full-time self-employment for many women, and the disruption to their trading and earning through displacement would have been detrimental to the economic survival of themselves and their families. The ages of the women also highlight the concern that a regulation or ban would have on those who were already struggling. When the registry was compiled in 1928, 80 per cent were between the ages of 18 and 59 years, prime years for working and supporting a family. The average age when a woman started trading, across all 147 traders, is 20 years; the youngest began trading at 11 years, and the oldest at 55 years. These figures indicate that street trading may have been the only work these women had ever done. Thus, a threat to trading and earning would likely put them at a further disadvantage of finding employment in an economy where they were already at a disadvantage.

This information is particularly poignant considering the length of time many women had been trading. Information in the registry records the trader with the least experience as having only been trading two months. The trader with the most experience had been trading 50 years. Approximately 86 per cent, or 126 women, then, had been trading to earn for more than five years. The length of time trading, and the corresponding time frame, is compiled in Table 1 in order to align the information provided by the sample with the larger, dominant narrative about the recent increases in the number of street traders in Cork.

Table 1. Years trading and era when entered trade

How long trading?	Number of traders/ % of total (147)	Era when entered Trade (approx.)
5 years or less	21 (14%)	1923–1928
6–10 years	23 (16%)	1918–1922
11–20 years	42 (29%)	1908–1917
21–30 years	28 (19%)	1898–1907
31–40 years	19 (13%)	1888–1897
40 years or more	14 (9%)	1887 and earlier

Source: 1928 List of Street Traders and Stall Holders, Cork City and County Archives.

The information provided by the Shawlies indicates that the period 1898 through to 1917 was when a significant number of these women commenced trading, figures that correspond to the trend noted in the second chapter. It is significant that 103 women had been trading for more than 11 years: this means that 70 per cent of the women registered in 1928 had been trading for more than a decade to support themselves and their dependents, or were contributing to the economy of a working-class family. Some had done so for as many as five decades, starting in 1878. As noted in the first chapter, the local authority had, two decades earlier, exempted Corn Market Street from charges of obstruction to facilitate trading; approximately 61, or 42 per cent, of these women would have started trading in the era when that exemption was established. To further put these numbers into historical perspective, only 14 per cent of the women trading started trading in the period 1923–8, the period that coincides with the foundation of the state, the passing of the Street Trading Act in 1926, and its introduction in Cork in 1928. In the period 1918–22, 16 per cent of the sample started trading. This is the period that coincides with the Anglo-Irish War, the Irish Civil War, and the increased momentum in calls by business interests to have street trading banned. Thus, 30 per cent of the women began trading during the period when war, displacement, uncertainty, national economic challenges and cuts to social welfare presented increased survival challenges for poor Irish women.

The address of each woman was recorded in 1928, and confirms that they were drawn from Cork's impoverished population. The residence information for these women is compiled in Table 2 according to the DED information available in the 1911 census. Four of the addresses could not be located in trade directories, maps, or in the 1911 census, and these four traders were removed from the sample for this analysis.

Table 2. Stall traders – residence according to DED

Cork DED	Number of traders residing in DED/% of sample (143)
Cork No. 1 Urban, No. 3 Urban, No. 4	3 (2%)
Cork No. 4 Urban	12 (9%)
Cork No. 5 Urban	8 (6%)
Cork No. 2	30 (21%)
Cork No. 7	35 (25%)
Cork No. 7 Urban	43 (32%)
Cork No. 7 Urban (part of)	7 (5%)

Source: 1928 List of Street Traders and Stall Holders, Cork City and County Archives.

While the specifics of the housing conditions they lived in in 1928 are not known, their residence in these areas provides some indication: these women, like their predecessors detailed in the following section, numbered among Cork's urban poor looking to earn a subsistence living. Unfortunately, not only were their livelihoods threatened by regulation, but so too were those of the women who would be their successors: correspondence from the Garda chief superintendent in Cork, dated 31 December 1928 and provided in the second chapter, indicated that Monahan had intended to limit the number of licences to existing traders.

SHAWLIE STORIES: 1901–28

Without additional information in the registry it is not possible to gather a richer picture of the lives of these women. Dates of birth were not provided, which makes precise information based on age difficult to assess and hinders gathering more information about these particular women from the 1911 and 1901 census returns. Taking into consideration factors such as a change in surname or transience, it is difficult to pinpoint women from this registry in the census returns compiled 17 and 27 years earlier. That said, close matches for seven of the 147 women emerge from both the 1911 and 1901 censuses. The following paragraphs traces their lives.

Bridget Coleman was a mother and a widow who earned a living as a clothes dealer according to both the 1901 and 1911 censuses, and her story appears in the narrative in the first chapter. In 1901, Bridget was illiterate and her three children were in school. In 1911, she was residing with her son, daughter, son-in-law and two grandchildren. In 1928, Bridget Coleman, 64, was living in the Corporation Buildings near Corn Market Street, and she was selling fish and fruit on Corn Market Street from a stall made of boxes and boards. She declared that she had been a trader for 45 years, making her approximately 17 years of age when she started.

In 1901, Mary Costello, aged 32, was a vegetable vendor and her husband, Patrick, was a coal porter; they lived at 9 Coach Street. In 1911, Mary Costello, aged 40, was living at 18 Portney's Lane, and was selling fish. At that time she was living with her husband of 20 years, Patrick, a general labourer; they lived with two cousins, one a general labourer and one unemployed, and her widowed aunt, aged 50 years, also a fish dealer. In 1928, Mary Costello, aged 60, was still living at 18 Portney's Lane, and was selling vegetables and fish on Corn Market Street from a stall made of boxes and boards. She reported that she had been a trader for 40 years, making her approximately 20 years of age when she started.

In 1911, only one woman named May Desmond appears in the census returns from Cork. At that time she was aged 22 years, and living in an apartment with two single aunts, aged 60 and 56 years, who were not working. May was a machinist. She was born in Dublin city. In 1928 a May Desmond, aged 40, lived at 20 James Street. She was selling boots and old clothes on Corn Market Street from a stall made of boxes and boards. She had been a trader for 18 years, making her approximately 22 years of age when she started trading.

In 1901, Margaret Hurley, aged 31, lived at 22 Cockpit Lane with three daughters, all in school. She recorded her occupation as charwoman. In 1911 a woman named Margaret Hurley, aged 44, was living at 22 Cockpit Lane. A widow, she was the head of the household and recorded her occupation as charwoman; she was illiterate. She resided with two daughters; one employed as a weaver, and the other as a factory hand. In 1928, Margaret Hurley, aged 62, lived at 23 Cockpit Lane and was selling fruit and fish on Corn Market Street from a stall made of boxes and boards. She had been a trader for 30 years, making her approximately 32 years of age when she started trading.

In 1901 Mary Kickham, aged 24, was married but did not live with her spouse. She was the head of the family and her profession was listed as housekeeper. She lived at 19 Harpur's Lane with her 2-year-old son and her mother. Mary and her mother were illiterate. In 1911, a woman named Mary Kickham, aged 32, lived at 14 Grattan Street. She was a widow and a mother of four children. A profession is not listed for Mary; she could read and write. In 1928, Mary Kickham, aged 50, lived around the corner from Grattan Street at 11 Henry Street, and she was selling old clothes in North Main Street from boards on the street. She had been a trader for 25 years, making her approximately 25 years of age when she started trading.

In 1911, a woman named Catherine McCarthy, aged 34, was a wool dealer. She was married to Michael, an upholsterer, and they lived with four children. Catherine had given birth to nine children who were living at birth, thus five of her children did not survive childhood. They lived at 24 Corporation Buildings at the top of Corn Market Street. In 1928, a Catherine McCarthy, aged 50, lived at 18 Cockpit Lane and was selling fish and vegetables on Corn Market Street from a stall made of boxes and boards. She had been trading for 25 years, making her approximately 25 years of age when she started trading. An entry for Catherine McCarthy does not appear in the 1901 census.

In 1911, Jane Sullivan, aged 36, was living at 8 Harpur's Lane with her husband, a fisherman; she declared her profession to be a dealer. Her 17-year-old daughter Ellen was also a dealer. Jane and Ellen could read but could not write. She had two younger children in school; Jane had given birth to four children who were living at birth, thus one did not survive childhood. In 1928, a Jane Sullivan, aged 50, was living at 22 Paul Street and was selling vegetables on Corn Market Street from a stall made of boxes and boards. She had been trading for 30 years making her approximately 20 years of age when she started trading. An entry for Jane Sullivan does not appear in the 1901 census.

In 1936, approximately nine years after the registry was completed, and the year before talk of the Street Trading Act, 1926, would resume in Cork, Seamus Murphy carved an image of the onion seller known as 'Mary Anne'. There is only one onion seller in the 1928 registry, but she was not itinerant like the woman Murphy had sculpted. She was Nellie Carlton, aged 23. She lived at 15 Brown Street and sold onions on Grand Parade from a stall made of boxes and boards. She had been trading for five years, making her approximately 18 years of age when she started trading. Only one Mary Anne appears in the 1928 registry. Mary Anne O'Sullivan, 70, was living at 22 Kyle Street and sold fish on Corn Market Street from a stall made of boxes and boards. She had been trading 50 years making her approximately 20 years of age when she started earning on the streets.

THE CALL TO REGULATE RESUMES

After the last correspondence received in 1929, advising that the issue of street trading in Cork would drop, the next entry in the by-laws file is from 1938 specifically in relation to Corn Market Street. The chief superintendent of An Garda Síochána in Cork wrote to Monahan to complain about street trading on Corn Market Street and the adjoining streets; the complaint was made in a letter dated 9 April 1938, and he indicated that the commissioner of An Garda Síochána had requested that Cork adopt the Street Trading Act, 1926, in order to deal with the situation. As an incentive, he reminded Monahan that the Corporation would be issuing licences that would generate revenue. The Musgrave Brothers Ltd are not mentioned in the complaint. It is known, however, that by the end of the 1930s they did, according to the *Irish Times*, have 'the edge on competitors': in that era the firm was, because of the Corn Market Street facility, wholesaling to grocers and retailers outside of Cork city as far away as Galway and Kilkenny.[11] No doubt that did stand to carry some political weight at all levels of governance, including the police.

Evidently, street trading had, at least on Corn Market Street, continued in the wake of Monahan's 'adoption' of the Act in 1928. It is clear, too, that Gardaí had not been prosecuting street traders there because they now had to ask for the Act's implementation. Monahan replied on 13 April 1938 and insisted that the Act was adopted in September 1928 and came into force the following January to target street trading in North Main Street. He indicated that that alone was sufficient to deal with the situation at the time, and no further action was taken. He advised he would contact the city solicitor to determine what needed to be done. It is clear, then, that not only had the Act not been given further thought after Monahan became city manager in 1929, there had been no further consideration as to how street trading would be regulated. The Shawlies had simply been moved off the streets where they were identified as a nuisance, contained at the loading area at the rear of the markets and away from the 'bricks and mortar' retailers. Then, on April 20, Monahan again wrote to the chief superintendent advising he would contact the Minister for Justice to obtain copies of regulations made elsewhere in the country, another indication that regulations had never been formally made. He asked for advice about the need to make by-laws under Section 6, despite having detailed regulations in the *Cork Examiner* in January 1929. On 27 April, the chief superintendent wrote back and advised Monahan that if street trading was to be dealt with successfully, the Corporation needed to make by-laws pursuant to Section 6 of the Act.

On 25 April 1938, the Minister for Justice forwarded the street trading regulations made in Bray in 1935. The following day, Monahan forwarded those to the city solicitor, advising that the chief superintendent wanted the Corporation to enforce the Act, adding 'We appear to have adopted the Act without taking steps to bring it into force'. He received a reply on 28 April, and was advised that regulations needed to be made by the Minister because the city's only control over street traders was limited to bringing charges of obstruction. The city solicitor advised that 'actual obstruction' was difficult to prove, adding, 'Justice always holds with us, but I have a certain amount of doubt in the matter', an indication that the sway of power must have been sufficient to register convictions against the women. Thus, despite Monahan's warnings to potential lawbreakers and threats of prosecution published in the *Cork Examiner* in 1929, nearly ten years later the only means of prosecuting the Shawlies in Cork was the charge of obstruction. When he next wrote to Monahan on 4 May, the city solicitor advised that nominating streets where stall trading is not allowed, as Monahan had done in 1929, was insufficient and by-laws were needed. More importantly, he reiterated that he had 'often' expressed the view that, 'as the law has stood hitherto, we had no right to prohibit stall trading' except under what he termed 'the very often fictitious ground of obstruction to traffic'.

It appears that the matter was then allowed to drop because the next item in the file is dated one year later. A memo from the town clerk in Cork to Monahan, dated 3 May 1939, provides a chronology of the Act's progress in Cork from 1928 through January 1929, noting no further entry in council minutes after that date. He added that the list of by-laws, dated May 1929, 'records that the Confirmation of the above by the Minister has been deferred'. On 6 May 1939, Monahan wrote to the city solicitor and asked that the Bray by-laws be returned because he had to address the matter again. Monahan then wrote to the town clerk on 9 May and asked if he could locate a letter from the Department of Local Government that approved the type of by-laws necessary, and if there was any further correspondence with that department dealing with them. The same day the town clerk wrote to Monahan and advised that the file of papers from the sitting in January 1929, when the Act was adopted, was missing. He added that he believed the correspondence from the Minister for Justice and the by-laws would be in the missing file.

This renewed activity on the issue may have been the result, again, of pressure from Gardaí: on 18 May, Monahan wrote to the chief superintendent in Cork and referenced previous correspondence and a visit to his office on the matter by a sergeant. He then wrote that the 'provisions' of the Street Trading Act, 1926, 'were adopted by me acting on behalf of the Cork Corporation on the 28th September 1929' revealing, again, an inconsistency with what was reported on in the *Irish Times* in July 1928. He added that 'the resolution passed at that time declared the Act to be in force in the County Borough of Cork as from the 1st January 1929'. He advised that it was necessary for the Minister for Justice to make regulations under section 13 of the Act, and that the Corporation then needed to make by-laws related to stall trading.

The council minutes of 27 June 1939 record that Monahan urged council to pass the by-laws. In keeping with construing street trading as disorderly, unhygienic and working counter to the workings of a 'modern' city, Monahan told the council that street traders were generating too much litter. The *Cork Examiner* covered this event on 29 June 1939 under a heading that implies criminal deviance: 'Illegal Trading'. The implication was that a law was in place: Monahan is quoted as saying that street trading was illegal, despite clearly knowing that there were no real laws governing street trading in Cork. However, he did qualify that it was not illegal under any existing laws against street trading, but was illegal under existing laws for obstruction. He then referred to the events of 1929, and alluded to an 'unofficial' arrangement made with traders to leave selected streets and congregate instead on Corn Market Street. He added that they were trading on Corn Market Street but without any legal right, despite the fact that the Corn Market Street was on the list of streets where he had approved street trading in 1929. He added that the Corporation could abolish street trading or, referring to the current situation, continue to ignore it.

At the council meeting on 27 July 1939 it was recommended that the draft by-laws be adopted but, according to the minutes, confirmation was postponed to accommodate proposed amendments at a later date. A handwritten note appears next in the by-laws file. Unsigned and undated, it is on the letterhead of the city manager and is situated between correspondence dated October 1939 and December 1939. It advises that complaints were received from 'certain shopkeepers regarding the type of structure now used for street trading at Corn Market Street'. The structures are described as resembling shops. The author goes on to say that 'the continued tolerances of the use of such structures for trading purposes constitutes a legitimate cause of complaint by shopkeepers'; it goes on to say that, without by-laws under the Act, what the author terms 'this abuse' could not be dealt with effectively. The author closes by suggesting that the Corporation reconsider the by-laws submitted at the meeting on 25 July 1939.

The role of business interests in regulating street trading in Cork, and their influence with Monahan on this matter, are indicated by the two pieces of correspondence that follow this note directly. The first is a letter from Monahan dated 9 December 1939, addressed to C.P. McCarthy, Incorporated Accountant. It begins by referring to a conversation they had earlier, and he writes that he

4. Coal quay tribute

has enclosed for McCarthy a copy of a report in advance of its presentation at the next meeting of the council. On 12 December, C.P. McCarthy, writing as the secretary of the Cork Master Bakers' Association, replied to Monahan. He indicated that he was grateful for both the letter and the copy of the report in advance of its presentation at council. He noted in closing that he had inspected the property in question and that it appeared to be permanent. He closed the letter by telling Monahan that he and several members of the association were grateful for his efficiency in dealing with the matter. At the council meeting on 12 December 1939, Monahan reported on the complaints about the new structure on Corn Market Street that was being used for street trading. He urged council to reconsider the street trading by-laws presented at the meeting on 25 July.

At the council meeting on 27 February 1940, the draft by-laws were approved. Corn Market Street was not on the list of prohibited streets, however the lanes adjoining Corn Market Street were, along with all remaining streets in the city centre. On 16 April 1940, Monahan wrote to the Department of Local Government and Public Health. He summarized events relating to the Street Trading Act, 1926, in Cork as follows: it was adopted in Cork on 28 September

1928; on 4 January 1929 draft by-laws were adopted and these were approved by the Minister for Local Government and Public Health in a letter dated 8 January 1929. He noted that while by-laws were made and submitted for approval, a confirmation was not issued because circumstances did not favour a broader enforcement of the Act at the time. He then requested ministerial approval for the new by-laws. There is no further correspondence on the issue.

The Street Trading Act, 1926, appears next in the public record on 24 November 1942. According to council minutes an alderman tabled a motion to request that the by-laws be revoked, alleging that 'unnecessary hardship' had been created for Cork's street traders. He said their trade was intergenerational and continuous 'for over one hundred and fifty years'. In that time, he said, their business had not been 'a hindrance or obstruction to traffic'. The motion was seconded, and the minutes simply record that a discussion followed and the motion was withdrawn. This event was not covered in the *Cork Examiner*, and there are no further entries in the by-law file. The Street Trading Act, 1926, or street traders do not appear again in the index of the council minutes.

THE 'MERCHANT CITY' MOVING FORWARD

This resurrection of the Act in Cork took place amid the writing and publication of the first officially commissioned town planning report, delivered in 1941. The language of this document echoed the language of modern efficiency in the planning documents of 1918 and 1926, and the discourse of efficiency emanating from the CPA in the early 1920s. According to the document's introduction, town planning was not about tearing down buildings to construct 'impossibly grandiose conceptions', but was a means of ensuring civic development on 'common sense lines'. The author – planning expert Robertson Manning – proposed that without planning overcrowding, 'ugliness, inconvenience' and 'useless expense' in 'compensation and services' would result. Manning wrote that there is nothing about town planning that should disturb the ratepayer,[12] putting the ratepayer, yet again, in a position of privilege over the citizen.

The medieval city centre where the Shawlies lived and worked was characterized as the 'decayed core', which required 'a policy of thinning out' to give it 'sun, light, and air'. Manning echoed the concern expressed in the *Survey* of 1926, and emphasized that there should be no rehousing in 'the Marsh', the neighbourhood on the north-east corner of the medieval city centre. He offered that, instead, the area would be better served by a 'public park, playgrounds, warehousing, market, etc.' The notion of the 'market' was not elaborated upon; he did, however, propose alternative uses for the existing markets – a central bus station was proposed, to be built on the site of the Bazaar Market and St Peter's Market. The displacement of existing stallholders in the Bazaar, or a new site for the sale of used clothing and affordable food and wares, was not included in the overall plan.

By the 1940s, the English Market had fallen into decline in line with the economic conditions of the day. Monahan was asked about the possibility of lowering the rents on the stalls; his reply says much about his attitude towards the Coal Quay. He advised that such a move would 'reduce' the English Market 'to the level of that of Corn Market Street'.[13] On 15 June 1946, a photo essay of Cork's landmarks and its power brokers, including a portrait of Monahan, was published in the *Irish Times*. Two photos appear side-by-side of the city's two major retail promenades, St Patrick's Street and Corn Market Street. This juxtaposition makes it clear that the emphasis on 'the modern', order, and hygiene continued towards the midpoint of the century. The caption described St Patrick's Street as 'fashionable' and 'orderly' with its 'modern shops', and Corn Market Street as a location marked by 'disorder, and the dirt that remains after each day's trading and bargaining'. The caption concludes: 'At Cornmarket [*sic*] you may pick up bargains, but you will spend a more tiring day there than you would in orderly Patrick street'.

In contrast, eight years later, the *Irish Times* ran an article on 2 October 1954 that described Corn Market Street as a world-renowned 'nostalgic spot', the 'subject of photographers looking for the quaint and the picturesque', and the 'object of curiosity for visitors'. Nostalgia was settling in as Corn Market Street was on the decline: the title of the article, 'Do you remember the Coal Quay?' hinted at what the article implied in the main, namely that this marketplace was possibly 'out of place in our new world of post-war mass-produced shiny things'. The traders interviewed said this was the case, suggesting that the glut of cheap goods available had compromised the second-hand trade. They stated that the Bazaar market was most lucrative when at its busiest, through the years of World War 1. The article questioned the market's future in strictly economic terms, observing that the Bazaar was not commercially viable to traders or the Corporation, and so its continued existence was in question. It was made clear that trading in these markets was intergenerational. The same decade, after persistently being cited as fiscal liabilities, both the Bazaar and St Peter's were targeted for demolition and redevelopment under a proposed scheme that included the conversion of St Peter's into a fire station or a basketball stadium.

Both the intergenerational nature of women trading on Corn Market Street and the market's future were explored again in an article in the *Irish Times*, dated 3 May 1985, entitled 'The market women of Cork'. This article stands out because it provides a rare opportunity to hear the voices of the women and their first-hand insights into the history of trading in their families. Trading was still a full-time occupation on the footpaths of Corn Market Street from Tuesday to Saturday, largely from stalls. Those interviewed are described as the 'real women of the Coal Quay'. Two women selling clothes claimed to have been 'nearly born' on the street, and were fourth-generation traders. Another, still selling fruit in her 70s, reported that she was part of a family of Shawlies who had traded there for approximately 150 years, a legacy that included her mother and her grandmother. In her words, 'The fruit was always our thing. It was passed on, like, that we'd sell the fruit. We never bothered with anything else'. However, despite the full-time nature of trade, and its intergenerational nature, it is clear that the open marketplace and street trading in the late 20th century was undergoing a transition. The reporter noted that those still trading claimed their daughters and granddaughters now refused 'to stand in the cold, week after week, selling vegetables or second-hand clothes'. This hints at both the physical challenges of the work, and the mental challenges of an uncertain custom.

One long-time trader reported that in the past the only women who sold on the street lived in the area; however, she reported that 'Now there's all kinds of tricky ones after coming along', referring to traders arriving from outside of Cork. She went on to recall more halcyon days for Corn Market Street, when meat was sold in St Peter's Market and, as a child, she would swing from the meat scales. A woman selling second-hand clothes reported that she was 'born and reared on the Coal Quay. We're here all our lives'. She described a street market where the stalls had once been 'four deep', with one side of the street consigned to the sale of eggs and poultry. She added that 'All the women wore shawls at that time'. This is much closer to the Corn Market Street of the old photographs: a vital marketplace with the ubiquitous presence of women covered in shawls. The article refers to the street's depiction in Bulfin's 1907 *Rambles in Eirinn,* detailed in the first chapter.

The strong community spirit described by Bulfin is notable, too, in the code the article describes the women used when sizing up a customer: 'H.B.' stood for 'heart breaker', someone of means haggling for the sake of haggling to bring down the return to the trader. In contrast, traders reported that they would, typically, reduce prices for someone who was genuinely poor. Despite the openness of this price mechanism, one customer claimed that consumer's tastes had now changed so that people had become fussy, and wanted their clothes to look like they came from 'Dunnes Stores'. She had been coming to buy in Corn Market Street since the age of two, a weekly visit that continued into her later years. The article alluded to changes in buying habits, calling the used-clothing market a 'Hippie' paradise in the 1960s and 1970s. These observations aside, the author noted that a market for used clothing still existed: on Saturday mornings women pushed prams stacked with used clothing to Kyle Street and sold from the prams, or piled the clothing on the street.

Much of the information in this newspaper article aligns with the data collected from the censuses and the registry. It is clear that trading was a full-time means of earning and living for women, and for many it was the only work they or their foremothers knew. It confirms that women specialized in particular commodities, and established custom in particular locations. Building on that data, it confirms that street trading was difficult work for little return, and earnings were vulnerable to changes in the larger economy and in Irish life. Thus, street trading was, historically, a very real means of earning for these women – it was not a lifestyle choice to earn 'pocket money', or a means of accumulating wealth outside of paying taxes or rates, despite what the negative meta-narratives surrounding street trading have claimed.

Nearly a decade later, on 28 March 1997, an article appeared in the *Irish Times* under the headline 'Expert warns on street traders' demise'. The expert was the European Union's General Secretary for Market Traders. He referred to Dublin's Moore Street and the prosecution of women selling on the street from prams as 'something from the Middle Ages'. He observed that the greatest threat to street markets anywhere in the EU was in Ireland. In the same article a representative of the Cork Corporation reviewed the history of Corn Market Street. He found that this street market was in decline, and was now operated only on weekends and daily during the Christmas season. He noted that the local authority had recently redeveloped it with financial assistance from the European Union, and it was becoming a successful market again. However, he said that he doubted if the market would operate seven days a week as it had in the past. He predicted that as a Friday and Saturday market it would be of value to the city. Ironically, more than 60 years after the local authority began coercing and containing the Shawlies, he also proclaimed that a market like the 'Coal Quay' was as much a part of Irish life as 'dancing, hurling or traditional butter-making'.

Eight years later, in May 2005, the Cork City Council adopted the *Cornmarket Street area action plan* that set 'an ambitious vision' for the transformation of the Coal Quay into 'a thriving urban quarter', one that would be 'attractive for business', and attractive to potential residents and visitors. The report identified the market in Corn Market Street as an active market since the late 18th century. However, the Cork City Council now called for a 'Street Market Strategy' to address the decline that followed the resurgence, described above, in the late 1990s. That resurgence had clearly ended: of the 371 market pitches available on Corn Market Street, only 140 were in use at the time of the report in 2004. According to the plan, an EU report blamed the decline of the street market on the movement of residents and businesses from Cork's city centre to the suburbs.[14] Ironically, the introduction of the action plan is accompanied by a photograph of a crowded Corn Market Street from a postcard taken in 1910, 14 years before the call to have street trading banned in Cork.

The social and political exclusion of the Shawlies evidenced by that ban continued, as indicated in the planning document of 1941. These exclusions aligned with the national picture as the review of certain key decisions that would negatively affect the poor and women, made by the government of William T.

Cosgrave, revealed. Contemporaneously, it is likely that the conditions created by these economic and social decisions forced a steady flow of Cork's poor and working-class women into street trading, along with the consumer demand among the urban poor for affordable necessities. The information contained in the 1928 registry confirms the Shawlies' need to earn by street trading. The information provided on the frequency of trading, number of years trading, and the age when these women started trading further develops their stories: clearly street trading was accessible to a woman at any age if she needed to earn. For some women it was the only work they had known during their lifetime, and for most it was a full-time occupation.

Conclusion

This study has attempted to fill in the 'gaps' in local history and lore about the Shawlies. They are among the women who have typically received little, if any, attention in studies of Irish history. The most significant gap filled is the 'emancipation', in some small part, of the stories of women street traders such as Mary Carlton and Bridget Coleman, along with the insight into the challenges that faced Mary Anne, Seamus Murphy's subject for the statue now known as 'the onion seller'. More broadly, this study has addressed how class and gender limited the agency of poor and working-class women in the decades that followed Irish independence. There is a body of work across disciplines on the larger political, economic and social policy decisions made by the government of William T. Cosgrave. However, the impact on these women of actions such as pension cuts, means testing for relief allocations, a failure to rigorously address unemployment, and ignoring the need for women to work has been brought into focus: their need to turn to trade or to continue trading was vital.

A question that emerged early in the study was why that same government took on these women street traders so early after the Anglo-Irish War and the Irish Civil War. Surely there were other more pressing concerns? However, the foundation of a state creates a socio-political climate that is likely to encourage 'power grabs', whereby various groups or interests try to push their agendas onto that of the new state. Clearly, the new Irish state experienced 'power grabs' by the DCA, the CTPA and the CPA. This was evident in their rush, so soon into independence, to lobby, successfully, for the dismantling of the local authorities, for urban planning that favoured commercial interests, and for the abolition of street trading in Dublin and Cork. More broadly, this study has brought into focus how the workings of those events would have consequences in the margins of the economy and society, far from centres of power, and how the workings of a seemingly innocuous piece of legislation, geared to be what leaders insisted was 'fair', created a hazard for women who needed to trade in the streets to ensure their survival and that of their families. This finding reveals how class and gender may also underpin urban planning – a seemingly innocuous programme of governance.

The more contemporary movements aimed at revitalizing Corn Market Street to its former 'glory' align with the trend in wealthy countries in the early 21st century to nostalgically resurrect open markets in city centres, as well as farmers' markets. Visitors to the regenerated Corn Market Street will notice that what is now labelled 'street trading' has little in common with the trade conducted by the Shawlies a century earlier. Just as the Act served the gentrification of streets and neighbourhoods it also, in part, gentrified retail trading by encouraging it to move indoors, and through privileging the voices of 'bricks and mortar' traders. What is now sanctioned in Ireland as 'street trading' aligns more closely with the order of the 'modern' city than its ancestor. Correspondingly, a question remains surrounding the likelihood that itinerant traders would be welcomed in these new spaces in Cork. In light of this study, that likelihood is questionable.

In 2010, a group calling itself 'Cork Shawlies Forever' formed to lobby the Cork City Council to have a Shawlie memorial erected on the Coal Quay. In December 2016, writing on the Facebook page 'Cork Shawlies Forever', the man leading that effort reported that despite a motion being passed in 2011 by the Cork City Council, the support of local councillors, and Corkonians both at home and abroad, there had been no further movement on the memorial although the improvements to the area had been completed. People in Cork have, since 2012, publicly celebrated these women and their custom annually on the opening day of Cork Heritage Week at the Coal Quay Family Festival. That festival opens with a Shawlies Parade. Unfortunately, however, it appears that an official and permanent recognition of the contribution made to the life and history of Cork city by the Shawlies has not materialized. The ubiquity of the Shawlies in local memory is evidenced in the fact that a chapter in Michael Lenihan's book bearing the title *Pure Cork* is devoted to the Shawlies. According to Lenihan, Cork's last Shawlie, Mary Ellen Lowther, died in 2010 aged 90 years. Lenihan writes that 'with her died an old Cork custom'.[1]

Notes

ABBREVIATIONS

CCCA   Cork City and County Archives
CE   *Cork Examiner*
CICCS   Cork InCorporation Chamber of Commerce and Shipping
CPA   Cork Progressive Association
CTPA   Cork Traders' Protective Association
DCA   Dublin Citizens' Association
DED   District Electoral Divisions
HCC   Hackney Carriages Committee
IT   *Irish Times*
TMC   Tolls and Markets Committee

INTRODUCTION

1 Cork town planning association, *Cork: a civic survey* (Cork, 1926), pp 14–15.
2 D. Ó Drisceoil, and D. Ó Drisceoil, *Serving a city: the story of Cork's English Market* (Cork, 2011), p. 45.
3 C. Clear, *Social change and everyday life in Ireland, 1850–1922* (Manchester, 2007), p. 37.
4 M. Luddy, *Women in Ireland, 1800–1918: a documentary history* (Cork, 1995), p. 157.
5 J. Bourke, *Husbandry to housewifery: women, housework and economic change, 1890–1914* (Oxford, 1993).
6 Clear, *Social change and everyday life in Ireland, 1850–1922*, p. 26.
7 R. Rhodes, *Women and the family in post-famine Ireland: status and opportunity in a patriarchal society* (New York, 1992), p. 126.
8 Clear, *Social change and everyday life in Ireland, 1850–1922*, p. 37.
9 Rhodes, *Women and the family in post-famine Ireland: status and opportunity in a patriarchal society*, p. 126.
10 F.W. Powell, *The politics of Irish social policy, 1600–1900* (New York, 1992), p. 172.
11 J.J. Lee, *Ireland, 1912–1985: politics and society* (Cambridge, 1989), p. 126.
12 M. O'Mahony, *Famine in Cork City: famine life at Cork Union Workhouse* (Cork, 2005), p. 41.
13 C. Stansell, *City of women: sex and class in New York, 1789–1860* (Urbana, IL, 1986).
14 M. Companion, 'Commodities and competition: the economic marginalization of female food vendors in northern Mozambique', *Women's Studies Quarterly*, 38:3&4 (2010) 163–81.
15 CCCA, HCC minutes, 27 Oct. 1902.
16 M. Foucault, 'Power and strategies' in C. Gordon (ed.), *Power/knowledge: selected interview and other writings, 1972–1977* (New York, 1980), pp 134–45.
17 M. Luddy and C. Murphy, '"Cherchez la femme": the elusive woman in Irish history' in M. Luddy and C. Murphy (eds), *Women surviving* (Dublin, 1992), p. 1.
18 F. Tonkiss, 'History of social statistics and the social survey' in C. Seale (ed.), *Researching society and culture* (London, 2004), pp 84–90.
19 T. Palys, *Research decisions: quantitative and qualitative perspectives* (Scarborough, ON, 2003), pp 252–3.
20 CCCA, HCC minutes, 16 Sept. 1924.
21 *CE*, 25 Sept. 1924.

22 The background of the statue, including her name, is found at http://www. adams.ie/Seamus-Murphy-RHA-1907-1975-Mary-Anne-The-Onion-Seller-1937-Bronze-91cm-high-35-8-high-Signed-and-inscribed-with-title-on-base-Provenance-From-the-Estate-of-the-late-Charlie-Hennessy-Cork-Literature-S?view=lot_detail. Accessed 1 Sept. 2016.

1. 'A CHAOS OF SITTINGS, STANDINGS, AND STALLS': THE SHAWLIES IN CORK'S RETAIL CORE AND PERIPHERY

1 J. Cross, 'Street vendors, modernity and postmodernity: conflict and compromise in the global economy', *International Journal of Sociology and Social Policy*, 20:1/2 (2000), 29–51.
2 S.F. Pettit, *This city of Cork, 1700–1900* (Cork, 1977).
3 CCCA at www.corkarchives.ie/merchantcity/home/merchantprinces. Accessed 1 Sept. 2016.
4 A. O'Callaghan, *Cork's St Patrick's Street: a history* (Cork, 2010), p. 34.
5 Ó Drisceoil and Ó Drisceoil, *Serving a city*, p. 43.
6 O'Callaghan, *Cork's St Patrick's Street*, p. 75.
7 Ó Drisceoil and Ó Drisceoil, *Serving a city*, p. 78.
8 Ibid., p. 54.
9 Ibid., p. 137.
10 Quoted in ibid., p. 88.
11 Quoted in ibid., p. 91.
12 M. Murphy, 'Cork commercial society 1850–1899' in L.M. Cullen and P. Butel (eds), *Cities and merchants: French and Irish perspectives on urban development, 1500–1900* (Dublin, 1986), pp 233–4.
13 G. Johnson and Cork, *The laneways of medieval Cork: study carried out as part of Cork City Council's major initiative* (Cork, 2002).
14 W. Bulfin, *Rambles in Eirinn, vol. 2* (London, 1981).
15 S. Beecher, *The story of Cork* (Cork, 2007), p. 106.
16 M. Lenihan, *Pure Cork* (Cork, 2010), pp 170–80.
17 CCCA, HCC minutes, 13 Oct. 1902 to 5 July 1915.
18 Ó Drisceoil and Ó Drisceoil, *Serving a city*.
19 Bulfin, *Rambles in Eirinn, vol. 2*.
20 Ó Drisceoil and Ó Drisceoil, *Serving a city*.
21 CCCA, TMC minutes, 20 Apr. 1910 to 1 Nov. 1916.
22 Ibid.
23 Murphy, 'Cork commercial society 1850–1899', pp 233–4.
24 D. White, *A history of Musgrave: the first 125 years* (Cork, 2001).
25 Ibid., p. 31.

2. 'A VERY DISTINCT INTEREST IN HAVING ORDER KEPT IN THE STREET': THE SWAY OF THE 'SMALLER MEN'

1 CCCA, HCC minutes, 19 July 1915 to 11 Dec. 1929.
2 CCCA, Cork City Council minutes, 12 Nov. 1920 to 28 Dec. 1923.
3 CCCA, HCC minutes, 19 July 1915 to 11 Dec. 1929.
4 CCCA, Cork City Council minutes, 12 Nov. 1920 to 28 Dec. 1923.
5 CCCA, HCC minutes, 19 July 1915 to 11 Dec. 1929.
6 CCCA, Cork City Council minutes, 12 Nov. 1920 to 28 Dec. 1923.
7 A. Quinlivan, *Philip Monahan, a man apart: the life and times of Ireland's first local authority manager* (Dublin, 2006), p. 59.
8 Copies of these documents, obtained from the National Archives of Ireland, appear as appendices in C.M. O'Shea, 'The introduction of the management system to local government with special reference to Cork city and Philip Monahan' (MA, University College Cork, 1995), 126–8.
9 A. Quinlivan, *Philip Monahan, a man apart*, p. 59.
10 D. White, *A history of Musgrave*.
11 CCCA, Law and Finance Committee minutes, 22 Mar. 1922 to 11 Dec. 1924.
12 CCCA, HCC minutes, 19 July 1915 to 14 Nov. 1929.
13 CE, 17 Sept. 1924.
14 CCCA, HCC minutes, 19 July 1915 to 14 Nov. 1929.
15 CE, 25 Sept. 1924.

16 CCCA, HCC minutes, 19 July 1915 to 14 Nov. 1929.

17 CCCA, TMC minutes, 16 Sept. 1924 to 14 Nov. 1929.

18 Quoted in O'Shea, 'The introduction of the management system to local government with special reference to Cork city and Philip Monahan', p. 31.

19 CCCA, TMC minutes, 16 Sept. 1924 to 14 Nov. 1929.

20 Street Trading Bill, 1925, second stage. 19 Jan. 1926, Dáil Éireann debate vol. 14. no. 1.

21 Private business, Street Trading Bill, 1925, fourth stage, 4 Feb. 1926, Dáil Éireann debate vol. 14. no. 5.

22 Oral questions, street trading in Dublin, 16 Feb. 1927, Dáil Éireann debate vol. 18. no. 16.

23 The correspondence and memoranda related to the Street Trading Act, 1926, is found in CCCA by-laws file no. CP/FILES/41.

3. 'WE'RE HERE NEARLY ALL OUR LIVES': DOCUMENTATION AND DISPLACEMENT OF THE SHAWLIES

1 Lists of street traders and stallholders in Cork, 1928, found in CCCA by-laws File No. CP/FILES/4, and available at http://www.corkarchives.ie/merchantcity/media/CP_List_of_Street_Traders_1928.pdf. Accessed 1 Sept. 2016.

2 T. Garvin, *Preventing the future: why was Ireland so poor for so long?* (Dublin, 2004), p. 29.

3 C. Meehan, *The Cosgrave party: a history of Cumann na nGaedheal* (Dublin, 2010).

4 M. Considine and F. Dukelow, *Irish social policy* (Dublin, 2009).

5 Lee, *Ireland, 1912–1985*, p. 126.

6 Quoted in C. Ó Gráda, *Ireland: a new economic history, 1780–1939* (Oxford, 1994), p. 91.

7 Ibid.

8 M. Jones, *These obstreperous lassies: history of the Irish Women's Workers Union* (Dublin, 1988).

9 Ibid., p. 87.

10 Considine and Dukelow, *Irish social policy*, p. 27.

11 *IT*, 11 Oct. 2006.

12 R. Manning, *Cork town planning report* (Cork, 1941).

13 Quoted Ó Drisceoil and Ó Drisceoil, *Serving a city*, p. 169.

14 *Cornmarket street area action plan (Section 4)*, (Cork, 2005). Available at http://www.corkcity.ie/services/strategicplanningineconomicdevelopment/localplanning/nonstatutoryplansand developmentbriefs/cornmarketstreet areaactionplan/July%202005%20 Section%204.pdf. Accessed 23 Sept. 2015.

CONCLUSION

1 Lenihan, *Pure Cork*, p. 170.